GREAT WAR
LIVES

FAMILY HISTORY FROM PEN AND SWORD

How Our Ancestors Lived

GREAT WAR LIVES

A Guide for Family Historians

Paul Reed

Pen & Sword
FAMILY HISTORY

First published in Great Britain in 2010 by
PEN & SWORD FAMILY HISTORY
an imprint of
Pen & Sword Books Ltd
47 Church Street
Barnsley
South Yorkshire
S70 2AS

ISBN 978 1 84884 324 0

A CIP catalogue record for this book is
available from the British Library.

Typeset in Palatino and Optima by
S L Menzies-Earl

Printed and bound in England by
the MPG Books Group, Bodmin, Cornwall

Pen & Sword Books Ltd incorporates the imprints of
Pen & Sword Aviation, Pen & Sword Maritime, Pen & Sword Military,
Wharncliffe Local History, Pen & Sword Select, Pen & Sword Military Classics
and Leo Cooper

For a complete list of Pen & Sword titles please contact
PEN & SWORD BOOKS LTD
47 Church Street, Barnsley, South Yorkshire, S70 2AS, England
E-mail: enquiries@pen-and-sword.co.uk
Website: www.pen-and-sword.co.uk

CONTENTS

ACKNOWLEDGEMENTS

First I would like to thank Rupert Harding, the commissioning editor of this title. I have very much enjoyed working with Rupert, who has always been willing to give good counsel and advice, and has made the work on the book so much easier.

As with all the books I have worked on, many old friends have offered help and assistance during this project. I would particularly like to mention Geoff Bridger, Maurice Johnson, Iain McHenry, Kyle Tallet (for great help with the Royal Naval Division), Teri Murphy, Pam Waugh and Wayne and Michelle Young. I would also like to thank all those friends on Facebook and Twitter who offered kind words of encouragement, and hope the book lives up to their eager expectations.

One friend, John Hayes-Fisher, deserves special mention. Having had the pleasure to work with John on numerous TV projects over many years, it has always been rewarding to stomp round a battlefield with him. For this book John very kindly gave up his time in a busy period to guide me round Wadhurst, and used his local knowledge to good effect.

Thanks to those who have given permission to quote from various publications and use images: David Langley for permission to quote from his excellent revised and annotated version of *Old Soldiers Never Die*; the Royal Engineers Museum for permission to use material on William Hackett; the West Sussex County Council Record Office for material from their regiment collection.

Peter Henderson, archivist at the King's School in Canterbury, was extremely helpful in sourcing material in the school's archives on Vernon Austin. I am indebted to him and his colleague Sarah Gray for answering my queries and allowing me to use the image of Austin's funeral. Kings now have a website featuring pupils who died in the Great War at: www.hambo.org/kingscanterbury/.

For information and photographs relating to William Hackett VC I am grateful to Jeremy Banning and Peter Barton for their help. They not only willingly shared their knowledge, but went out of their way to assist. To their credit they have been working on a memorial to Hackett, which should be in place at Givenchy by the time this book is published. Details of their project can be found at: www.tunnellersmemorial.com.

My sincere thanks go to members of the Great War Forum who have helped with many minor enquiries, which have helped to make up the larger picture. A few asked to remain anonymous, but I would especially like to thank Chris Baker, Terry Denham, Andy Lonergan, Ken Lees, Dave O'Mara, Andy Pay, Kim McMahon, Kate Wills and Joan Wilson. Joan Wilson's father, John Stephens, was exceptionally kind in providing a copy of the *History of the Royal Naval Division*, for which I am especially grateful.

Finally, as ever, a special thanks to my family: to my wife Kieron, and also Ed and Poppy, who have both followed me from childhood into being young adults on the many journeys to trace these Great War lives. Without all their love and support this book, and all the others, would not have been possible.

INTRODUCTION

Nearly a century ago, in August 1914, at the end of a golden summer Great Britain slipped into war. Dragged into that conflict were the lives of millions of men who would serve overseas as regular soldiers, territorials, wartime volunteers – and by 1916 – conscripts. More than ¾ million of them never returned, and many times that number were wounded, went sick or had their futures changed forever by what they had seen on the battlefields of the Great War. It was a conflict that affected the population in a way that no other war ever had, and the echoes of it in some ways continue to this day.

In thirty years of visiting the battlefields of the Great War, and researching those who fought on them, my work as an historian has uncovered many fascinating individuals. This book gives me the opportunity to tell a few of those stories, which for so long have deserved to be known by a wider audience. But of course no single volume, and certainly not one detailing the lives of just twelve men out of millions who served, could ever hope to completely portray the experience that was the Great War. But this book takes these twelve men and hopes to retell in part what the war was about.

How were these men selected, and why? Vernon Austin takes us to the early days of the war and the Battle of Mons, where the first shots were fired. His death in Northern France once the war had become stagnant reveals attitudes to the burial of the dead that would influence later policy, and see him being one of only a handful of fatalities who were repatriated home. The story of the Wadhurst Company from rural Sussex shows how just one day of battle could have a profound effect on a locally recruited unit, and for the first time highlights that arguably Wadhurst suffered proportionally more than any other community in Britain. The Great War was not just about big battles and the life and death of Greek Cypriot Ectos Maffuniades exposes the myth of 'all quiet on the Western Front'. In the same vein, a static war saw the re-introduction of old methods of warfare, and the experience of William Hackett VC sheds light on the often forgotten underground war beneath the Western Front.

Big battles are also important, as they in many ways define our view of the war, and the stories of Rifleman Frank Davies and Private Henry Penn tell the great tales of the Somme and Passchendaele, two names that continue to resonate down the ages. The Western Front wasn't the only theatre of war, and Coburn Cowper's three years abroad help explain fronts such as Salonika and Palestine. Aside from showing the naval involvement, Fred Stoneham's chapter exposes the sacrifice of men from the Royal Naval Division at Gallipoli in 1915. Life above the battlefield is seen through Robbie Clarke's service with the Royal Flying Corps – an even more important story as Clarke was the only Afro-Caribbean pilot to fly for Britain in the Great War.

Finally, it was important to see how the war affected men in different ways. Frank Plumb, mutilated by a shell fragment, became an early 'guineas pig' when he had his face rebuilt through plastic surgery. Ernest Hopcraft shows how soldiers could be complicated men, often walking a fine line between villain and hero. And Great War poet Ivor Gurney survived the war despite two wounds only to be tortured by his experience of it until his dying day, becoming as much a casualty of the war as those who fell in battle.

They are but twelve tales, yet among the twelve is the Great War in microcosm and hopefully the reader will find some insight into their own Great War family members, which is why at the end of each chapter there is an explanation of how the research for that story was conducted. This will point those interested in military genealogy in the right direction, and highlight some of the major sources used in any research into this subject.

The legacy of the Great War is all around us even if at times we barely notice it. It invades our speech with verbal currency from the trenches. Our landscape is sometimes dominated by its memorials. Streets bear the names of many of its most infamous battles and even now each year the nation comes together on a crisp November morning as local stone is splashed with the red of poppy petals. But the voices of that war have passed from us; they are silent now, with the death of Harry Patch, the 'last British Tommy'. But the echoes of him and so many other Great War lives go on. If life can have meaning then I hope this handful of stories will mean something to those who never met a man who went to war during those defining years of 1914–18, and bring into sharp focus a generation the like of which we shall probably never see again.

Paul Reed
www.battlefields1418.com
www.twitter.com/sommecourt
Kent and The Somme

A GUIDE TO
GREAT WAR RESEARCH

Although details of how the stories of the twelve men described in this book were researched are located at the end of each chapter, a short overall guide to the main sources available is found below. The Internet has made research a great deal easier, but many records are still not online, and may not be for some years to come, and in some respects nothing really substitutes for research in original documents. The majority of these undigitised records are located at The National Archives (TNA) at Kew, London, an archive open to all and a visit to which is highly recommended.

Starting Point – Medals

At first, with only a name and the smallest details, starting research on a Great War serviceman can seem daunting. The place to begin is always within the family; try to find their campaign medals, ask around for photographs and documents and speak to family members who may have some details. From there the Medal Index Cards should be used to research men in the Army. These can be seen on microfiche at TNA and online via

A Medal Index Card for a soldier who died in the war showing the typical information found in this source: military details and information on medals. (Michelle Young, Western Front Association)

Ancestry and TNA's Documents Online site. This will provide you with the basic details of the man concerned, and for the Army the next step would be to consult the Medal Rolls in WO329 at TNA. These normally provide the battalion for infantry soldiers, and for men who served in Corps, some other information is normally located here. Naval personnel are not found on the Medal Index Cards unless they were later commissioned in the Army, so the starting point for them are the Naval Medal Rolls in ADM171 at TNA. These are currently not online, but there are plans to make them available in 2010/11.

Did He Die in the War?

Having checked the serviceman's medal entitlement, did he die in the war? If so, the next step is to check his details on the Commonwealth War Graves Commission website at: www.cwgc.org. This site lists all those who died while serving in a military unit during the Great War, confirms their military details, occasionally gives additional information such as age and next of kin, and shows where they are buried or commemorated. The site also explains the fantastic work the Commission does worldwide in maintaining cemeteries and memorials. Further information can then be traced in *Soldiers Died in the Great War* (with a separate volume for officers), which is now available online via several sites such as Ancestry, FindMyPast and Military Genealogy. A digitised version was also produced on CD-ROM and is available at many reference libraries.

Service Records

Service records of ordinary soldiers in the Army were badly affected by bombing in the Second World War, and many were lost. These records were held for many years by the Ministry of Defence at Hayes. These were transferred to class WO363 at TNA and became known as the so-called 'Burnt Documents'. The Ministry of Pensions had also retained many records and these form class WO364, the so-called 'Pension Records'. At a conservative estimate together they probably account for less than 60 per cent of those who served, so there are many gaps. Both classes have been digitised and are available on Ancestry, but can also be consulted on microfilm at TNA. Officer's records are only available as original documents in WO339 and WO374 at TNA, with an index in WO338. Naval Records are in ADM188 and can be downloaded at Documents Online, along with service records of Royal Marines and men from the Royal Naval Division. None of the Admiralty papers were damaged in the Second World

Wartime photographs of soldiers in the possession of your family can help with research, and provide vital clues about units.

War, and remain complete. Royal Flying Corps and Royal Air Force records are available in AIR79, with RAF officer's records available at Documents Online.

Operational Records

All branches of the armed forces kept records of their movements and engagements during the war. In the Army and Royal Naval Division these were known as War Diaries. For the Army and some Royal Naval Division units they are in class WO95 at TNA. Many have now been digitised and can be downloaded from TNA's Documents Online for a small fee. A few of the Royal Naval Division diaries are in class ADM137, but mainly cover 1914–15 when the division was in Belgium and Gallipoli. Royal Navy ships kept Ship's Logs, but these are not as detailed as war diaries and have a low survival rate because many ships were lost at sea; surviving examples are in ADM53. Squadron records of units in the Air Force are in AIR1 but are far from complete, and for some no diaries exist at all. However, some Squadrons have published histories or privately published accounts exist, and it is worth contacting the RAF Museum to see what they have in their archives.

Army, Navy and Air Force Lists

The details of men who were commissioned as officers were published in Army, Navy and Air Force lists during the war. For the Army there were two types of Army List, a Monthly and a Quarterly one. The Monthly Lists contained every commissioned officer showing who he was serving with, often which battalion if he was in an infantry regiment, along with his rank and date of commission into that rank. Indexes make it easy to find a name. Quarterly Lists were also published and normally only contained regular Army officers, but featured much more information, especially in the January edition which had summaries of officers' war services. Navy Lists were monthly and showed rank and ships or shore stations attached to, along with dates of commission. Again they had an index, but there is no equivalent of the Army Quarterly Lists. Until 1 April 1918, when the RAF was created, officers from the Royal Flying Corps and Royal Naval Air Service were listed in the Army and Navy lists respectively. Thereafter, the Air Force List was created which contained details of all those commissioned in the RAF, showing rank and date of commission, but no information about what squadrons a man was attached to.

Honours and Awards

By the end of the Great War a whole collection of gallantry medals were available that could be awarded for brave and meritorious conduct on and off the battlefield. No award could be made without a written recommendation, but sadly these documents were lost in bombing during the Second World War. It therefore means that for most gallantry medals no form of 'citation' is available. However, details of all such medals were published in the *London Gazette* and for most awards, with the exception of the Military Medal and Meritorious Service Medal, a citation is usually shown. The *London Gazette* is available on microfilm at TNA and on the Internet at Gazettes Online. The online index can be tricky to use, and sometimes it is worth putting in the soldier's regimental number to find him. Pages are presented in PDF format and can be printed off and saved.

Rolls of Honour and Newspapers

Both during and after the Great War local Rolls of Honour were published in many locations across Britain. Schools, colleges, universities, factories, coal mines and even shops and insurance companies published details of those who served. Many featured biographies, obituaries and photographs and some contain considerable information not found in other sources. When the conflict was over one publishing company tried to take this further by producing 'The National Roll of the Great War'. The plan was to publish a volume for every town and city, but constraints of time and cost meant that only a handful was ever produced. While the 'National Roll' is now available online at sites such as Ancestry, very few other rolls of honour are. Some are found in the Project Guttenberg source for digitised books, but the majority can only be located in local study centres, county record offices, the Imperial War Museum and the Society of Genealogists' library.

Contemporary newspapers are a very much underused source for Great War research. In the early years of the war when censorship was virtually non-existent they contain a huge amount of information and usually include lists of local men serving, often along with photographs. Obituaries of local men killed at the front are found in these sources, and frequently letters from the front and information on those given gallantry awards. Some local newspapers still exist, and a call to their offices will ascertain whether they have any back issues available, normally on microfilm. The most complete collection is found at the National Newspaper Library at Colindale in North London, a part of the British Library. Local indexes enable the visitor to ascertain quickly what newspapers were published in their area.

Websites

The expansion of the Internet over the past decade has opened up Great War research in a way that was not previously possible. It has also resulted in literally hundreds of websites dealing with research, battles and battlefields, units and war memorials, to list but a few of the many themes reflected in sites. It is always worth remembering that Internet sites are un-edited and should always be treated with some caution, but some recommended sites are detailed below.

Commonwealth War Graves Commission: www.cwgc.org
The Commission website includes the 'Debt of Honour' Register, which lists all those who died in the Great War and where they are buried or commemorated. It is therefore a starting point for servicemen who died. The site also has details of every cemetery and memorial.

The Long, Long Trail: www.1914-1918.org
Chris Baker's site is arguably one of the most important on the Internet

from a Great War perspective. It includes details of every regiment and corps, every division and guides to many other aspects of the war. It should really be the starting point and reference guide to any form of Great War research on the Internet.

WW1 Battlefields: www.ww1battlefields.co.uk
Alan Jenning's site is well constructed and an excellent starting point and guide to visiting and researching the Great War battlefields with many useful links.

The Great War Forum: http://1914-1918.invisionzone.com/forums/index.php?
Created in 2002 and having thousands of members including many published authors, this is the site to visit if you have what you think are unanswerable questions on your research.

Geoff's Search Engine: www.hut-six.co.uk/cgi-bin/search1421.php
Geoff Sullivan has created a fantastic tool for researchers which enables you to search fully the Commonwealth War Graves Commission website, producing, for example, lists of men from specific regiments who died on a specific day, or producing a list of every man whose details include mention of a specific city, town or village.

Roll of Honour: www.roll-of-honour.com
A well-researched and truly massive website with details of British war memorials listing those who died. While it does not cover every location and every memorial, it is an important and useful site.

The Western Front Association: www.westernfrontassociation.com
Formed in 1980, the Western Front Association is a organisation for anyone with more than a passing interest in the Great War. It produces a high-quality journal and newsletter, and has branches all over the United Kingdom. The website is packed with information.

Museums

While few museums have records of individuals (a notable exception being the Guards Museum) they can be good sources of supplementary material, especially images. The break-up of county regiments since the 1960s has meant that many regimental collections have become fragmented. These are sometimes found in County Record Offices, but most regimental museums do have something, even if it is just a collection of photographs. The majority can be found online, and contact made. Remember that such institutions are often staffed by volunteers so be patient when waiting for a response, and if contacting them by mail, enclose an SAE.

Museums such as the Imperial War Museum, National Army Museum, Royal Air Force Museum and Naval Museum at Greenwich (all located in London) are useful to visit to gain a wider context but they all have archives and reading rooms, which can be useful in your own research. While they are unlikely to have details of your own relative, they may hold papers of a man who served with him, which would give useful background to the experience of those who served at the same time. They may also have photographic archives for general images connected with the places and battlefields on which he served.

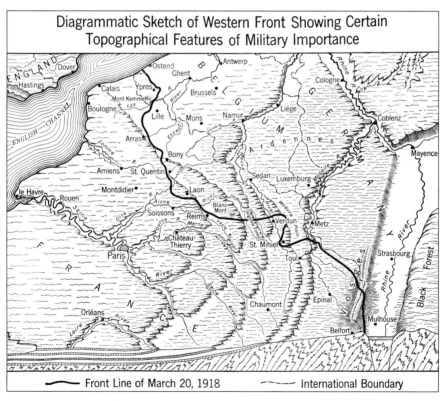

The Western Front, 1918.

Chapter One

THE BOY WHO CAME HOME

Lieutenant Vernon James Austin,
Royal Field Artillery

The years before the Great War saw a rise in the ownership of the motor car, something that is taken for granted a century later. One pioneer at the centre of this development was Sir Herbert Austin. Austin was born in Buckinghamshire, but grew up and was educated in Rotherham, Yorkshire. In the 1880s he was seduced by an uncle's stories of Australia and persuaded his mother to let him depart for Melbourne, where he became an engineer working on engines and machinery to aid in sheep-shearing. He married Helen Dron in December 1887, and they had three children: a son, Vernon, and two daughters. Vernon was only a few months old when the family moved to England, where his father began pioneering work on the development of a popular motor car. He took over an old print works at Longbridge, near Birmingham, a location that would become synonymous with the British car industry. By 1908 he had seventeen models in production, and the company was a success, earning Herbert a significant income. The market for these cars was not the working man; it would be several years before Austin cars were affordable to ordinary families. In the Edwardian period the market was clearly the rising middle classes and those in the upper echelon of society, like the Austins, as the average Austin car cost several hundred pounds; a small fortune prior to 1914.

As Herbert Austin's business flourished, his family was growing up as well. From their home outside Birmingham, Vernon left for school and was

Vernon Austin in pre-war dress uniform mounted on his charger.

initially educated at St Cuthbert's, Malvern, and in September 1907 went to the King's School in Canterbury. King's was a fee-paying boarding school, considered one of the finest in the country. Located in the centre of the city of Canterbury, the tower of the medieval cathedral was visible from the school grounds. But Canterbury in Edwardian times, as it is today, was a city of contrasts. Urban life could easily be exchanged for the rural idyll very quickly, as the countryside around the city was dotted with small villages, country lanes and hillside walks. Vernon developed a great love of Canterbury, and he was described by a master at the school as: 'always a quiet, reserved boy he spent his two years here in the Engineering Class, preparing to take his place in his father's Motor Car works, and perhaps few of his contemporaries knew his amiable disposition, his keen intelligence, and his grit'.[1]

Leaving the school in 1909, he went on to further education in Leipzig where he studied engineering. At this time the reputation of German universities among the English middle and upper classes was supreme, and although diplomatic relations between the two countries was strained even then, it gave Vernon an insight into a country that a few short years later Britain would be at war with.

On his return to England, Vernon's family were now living at Lickey Grange, Bromsgrove. This large rambling country house was a clear sign of Vernon's father's success. Now a young man, Vernon became increasingly interested in motor cars, and not just driving them round the lanes of rural Worcestershire. He became passionate about racing them as well. Motor racing, like the cars, was very much in its infancy at this time, but Vernon Austin may well have gone on to become one of its famous pioneers if he had survived the war. Indeed, in 1914, just at the world went to war, Vernon was set to depart for Russia to take part in a race there, but it was not to be. The hand of war brought the golden age of the Edwardian middle classes to an end.

While at King's School, Vernon had joined the School Cadet Corps. All schools like King's had such an institution where the boys of the school could learn the rudimentary elements of military service, duty and drill. It was often seen as a good grounding for a future career in the military. Vernon, however, given his wish to work for his father and pursue his interest in motor racing, had no such desire, but in late 1911 joined the Special Reserve of Officers. This was created in 1908 as a successor to the Militia; young men could agree to serve in the Army, undergo the required training, but it was not a full-time commitment. Aside from the training, regular periods of refresher training and camps, the individual was free to continue with their normal civilian life. The War Office paid the person concerned, but the catch was in time of war these men could be called up and would be able to go straight into the Army and immediately serve – being fully trained. For Vernon this was an ideal situation as he could fulfil the patriotic duties befitting someone of his class and background, and continue life in Edwardian Britain.

But Europe soon descended into war. On 4 August 1914 Britain declared war on Germany, and all those in the Special Reserve were called up for immediate service. Vernon had his commission in the Royal Field Artillery, and he was at once posted to the 22nd Battery, 34th Brigade Royal Field Artillery on 5 August. The 22nd Battery, and 34th Brigade, were one of three artillery Brigades in the 2nd Division. This regular Army infantry division had a number of support units, as was common in all such formations. As part of its complement there were three artillery brigades, to provide fire support. Each Brigade, like the 34th, was made up of three Batteries – like Vernon's 22nd Battery. A battery consisted of six field guns; in the case of

A British artillery brigade, equipped with 18-pounder field guns, during the Retreat From Mons, August 1914.

the 22nd these were the 18-pounder field guns, the standard field gun of the British Army at this time. Vernon was one of 198 officers and men in the battery, which was commanded by a major. In his role as a lieutenant, Vernon would have been responsible for a section of two guns in the Battery. While they were based in Aldershot, there was only a matter of days for Vernon to acclimatise to life as an artillery officer, get to know the men in his section and meet his fellow officers before the Battery departed for France. Loaded up at Southampton, Vernon disembarked at Le Havre on 17 August 1914, less than two weeks since he had been mobilised.

With the guns unloaded they were limbered up, each limber pulled by four horses. On horseback, riding his own mount, Vernon would have accompanied his gun section along the cobbled roads of France as they pulled out of Le Havre. Their orders came down from Divisional Headquarters, and were simple but direct; 'The Division would move on the morrow towards its allotted place in the line of battle.'² This took Vernon and his gunners along the Roman roads in Northern France, through many small towns and villages where the French locals greeted them with cheer, but no doubt with a slight look of nervousness. Finally, on the 21st they reached the Belgian border, and crossed into the country for which Britain had gone to war a few weeks earlier. Their destination was the small village of Givry, only a few miles beyond the border.

Givry was south-east of the city of Mons, where the commander of the British Expeditionary Force (BEF), Sir John French, had decided to concentrate the assembling units of the BEF while he ascertained exactly where the advancing German forces were located and what the plans of his French counterparts might be. Britain had been prepared for war in 1914, and a plan to mobilise an expeditionary force of several infantry divisions, cavalry, artillery, engineers and support troops and bring them across to the continent had been formalised several years before. It has been successfully put into place, and, as per plan, French had taken the BEF to a point just west of the main French army. While shipping to get the BEF to France had not been a problem, moving it from the ports to the front line had been. Little rail transport was available and units like the 22nd Battery had had to make their own way to the battle front.

Upon arrival, the six guns of the 22nd Battery were dug in just east of the Givry–Mons road. The front line was just under 3,000yd ahead of them at Vellereul le Sec, where the men of the 1st Royal Berkshires and 1st King's Royal Rifle Corps were in hastily prepared firing trenches. While this may seem like a long way, the effective range of Vernon's 18-pounders was more than 6,500yd, and up to 7,800yd when dug in, as they were here. Field guns largely fire indirectly; over a battlefield and on to a target beyond. The gunners manning the artillery pieces cannot possibly see targets over that sort of distance, so one of Vernon's jobs was to establish an Observation Post (OP) at a vantage point that overlooked the battlefield and front line, where he could see the enemy forces and link that OP via a static telephone line, provided by the signallers in his section. As the gun teams dug in, Vernon went off across the fields on horseback and found a suitable site for the OP on the rising ground towards Vellereul. With 176 rounds per gun at the gun sites, more than 800 per gun available from the Divisional Ammunition column, all was set for the first engagement.

On the morning of 23 August 1914 the Battle of Mons began and Vernon and his gunners saw action for the first time. For the infantry he was supporting in the front line it was a fairly quiet day. They saw no direct sign of the units of 18th Infantry Division advancing towards them, but instead witnessed the harassment of their own artillery by the German guns: 'Enemy's artillery opened fire . . . and searched the ground all round our artillery, kept up for about 1 ½ hours. Got a little sleep [until] enemy opened artillery fire again on our artillery, but not on infantry trenches.'[3] Incredibly, the 22nd Battery came through unscathed but a sister battery in the Brigade lost two officers and ten men.[4] It was an odd sort of day, as the divisional historian recorded:

When darkness fell on the 23rd the 2nd Division had done little or no fighting. Casualties certainly were sustained, but excepting artillery duels, the Division cannot be said to have joined action with the enemy. The casualties were caused mainly by the artillery fire of the enemy, who searched the ground thoroughly over which his infantry was to advance.[5]

But the position had been held and no ground given up. It therefore came as something of a surprise the following day when Major General C.C. Monro, commanding 2nd Division, received instructions from Sir John French to begin a withdrawal. Monro discovered that his chief had received a telegram from General Joffre, his counterpart in the French army, that the Belgian town of Namur had fallen and the French Fifth Army had evacuated Charleroi. On both of Sir John's flanks French forces were pulling back, and he had no choice to do likewise, or risk being surrounded and wiped out. The Retreat from Mons had begun.

Vernon James Austin, 1914.

Vernon and his gunners at Givry no doubt received the orders with some surprise. They were soon to discover their departure was not immediate, as the field guns of the division were to cover the withdrawal of the infantry. On the morning of the 24th they opened fire at 4.45 am, and this continued into the late morning as the infantry got away. Gun sites were then abandoned, equipment checked and guns limbered, and Vernon's section was on the road again with the rest of the Battery. Several problems faced Sir John's men on this retreat. The roads in the area suitable for the sort of transport an artillery battery required were limited. It had been manageable on the way up, but now in the hour of retreat the roads were crowded with men and equipment of every type of unit. Spending a night in the nearby town of Bavai, where the Battery once again guarded the withdrawal before moving off, the next obstacle was the mass of the Mormal Forest. This huge area of woodland split the British Expeditionary Force (BEF) in two, with Lieutenant General Haig's I Corps, of which the 2nd Division was a part, using roads and tracks to the east of it, and Lieutenant General Smith-

Dorrien's II Corps to the west. On the 26th as the 22nd Battery was crossing the Sambre River, and as the Retreat was going well, Smith-Dorrien's Corps stood and fought at Le Cateau. The noise of that battle would have been heard by Vernon and his men, but on they went. The Retreat from Mons would take them along the roads of France on a journey the equivalent of going from Louth to London. For days there was no fighting, only endless slog. For the gunners of the 22nd Battery life was easier than for the infantry, who were on foot; at least they travelled by limber or on horseback. The divisional historian recalled that the long line of troops were,

> sleep-starved men, almost dropping from fatigue; of miles trudged uncomplainingly along hot, dusty roads; of broken nights and early morning startings before the sun had risen. Proud in the knowledge that whenever he had joined action with the enemy he had beaten him off, and had inflicted far heavier losses than he had suffered, the British soldier did not question the reason why he continually had to retire; it was an order, and, as such, to be obeyed.[6]

Finally, on 5 September this long march came to an end. After 236 miles the BEF re-assembled close to Paris around the River Marne. Vernon and those in the 22nd Battery found themselves on the move again, this time in the opposite direction. The 'Miracle of the Marne', when Joffre's army had stopped the Germans almost at the very gates of Paris, had pushed the invader back. The Germans were now in retreat from the Marne to the Aisne and the men of the BEF were in hot pursuit. The 22nd Battery came into action again on 14 September at Verneuil, on the slopes of the Aisne heights where it engaged targets around Malval Farm on the high ground of the Chemin des Dames. The Battery War Diary records that in return they came under howitzer fire, which particularly affected the wagon lines. The fighting merged into the 15th, and the enemy counter-battery fire continued, scoring a direct hit on one gun, killing not only many of the crew, but also Vernon's commanding officer, Major Hugh Talbot Wynter. Wynter was a 41-year-old career soldier with a grown-up family – his eldest son would serve at sea before the end of the war – who had served in many campaigns during more than twenty years as a soldier.[7] Another officer was killed the same day, along with several other gunners and signallers. Artillery batteries were so small that the loss of so many in just a few days would have been a shock to the survivors like Vernon. He and the handful of officers left had to pull together to ensure the men's morale ran high. No doubt they occupied them with work, as after the fighting for the heights both sides had now dug in and the 22nd Battery began to prepare proper gun positions in a new location at Courtonne Farm. Here they would remain for the next few weeks until the fighting took them north, to Flanders.

In mid-October 1914 Vernon and the men of the 22nd Battery, now commanded by Major Washington, found themselves on the move again. This time they were being transported by train. Passing from the scenic countryside of the Aisne and the Marne, they moved across the rolling downs of Picardy into the flat landscape of Northern France with its coalfields and small industrial towns. Unloading at Hazebroucke, they followed the roads to the border and found themselves in Belgium once more. Their route and the maps they were issued with were taking them to a small Flemish town whose name would come to stand for the sacrifice of the Western Front: Ypres. On the 20th they were billeted in the town; it was very different then to later. There was little damage to the buildings, although the fighting that became known as the First Battle of Ypres had already started, and the local civilian population was still there, attempting to go about their usual business. The Germans were now advancing on the Channel ports in the so-called 'Race to the Sea' to try and isolate France by the capture of its vital link to the outside world. Flanders stood in the way, and now the Belgians, British and French were defending this ground. The 22nd Battery moved up to a small hamlet called Frezenberg, on some rising ground north-east of Ypres. Here they dug in and fired in support of the infantry defending the slit trenches around the village of Zonnebeke, a position and a role they would occupy for the rest of the battle. Compared to the disaster on the Aisne, there were only a handful of casualties here and staying in one position meant that Vernon would have returned to his role of establishing an OP so that his guns could fire more effectively.

In late November 1914 the 2nd Division, 22nd Battery along with them, pulled out of Flanders and went south to the trenches of Northern France. The days of movement and advance were coming to an end. The German army had been stopped at Ypres, and across the border between Armentières and La Bassée, but both sides had dug in. The primitive slit trenches of the Aisne and First Ypres was rapidly giving way to a whole network of proper trenches. Over the course of the winter of 1914/15 this infrastructure grew, creating what became known as the Western Front: 450 miles of trenches stretching from the Belgian coast to the Swiss border. Artillery would take on a major role during this static period of trench warfare, as both sides used shell fire to pummel a distant, well-entrenched enemy.

An 18-pounder gun team at their weapon. Vernon Austin commanded a section of these guns in 1914.

The 2nd Division relieved Indian troops in December 1914 around the village of Richebourg l'Avoué. This was a very flat area of the front line in Northern France, with the only high ground beyond the German trenches on the Aubers Ridge. The British trenches stranded a section of road called the Rue de Bois, with the gun positions located just north of the road towards the village of Richebourg proper. Several brick-built houses along the Rue de Bois offered vantage points for observation officers like Vernon to get a view of the German trenches, and over the course of Christmas and New Year his Battery was in support of the 1st Battalion King's Royal Rifle Corps (KRRC) in this sector of the battlefield. The War Diary of Austin's unit for the entire month of January only covers two pages, which indicates what a monotonous experience it was; the cold, snow and wet made major operations impossible. For the infantry it was a daily task just to survive the elements, but equally there were risks from shell fire, grenades, trench mortar weapons and also German snipers.

Flat ground with buildings looking out across the landscape is ideal ground for snipers. At this stage of the war the Germans had the upper hand in sniping, with German sniping teams active and the British not really having anything to counter them. On 24 January 1915 the 1st KRRC lost an officer from sniping activity – snipers would normally target officers as killing them caused the greatest damage to the enemy. It was clear that a sniper was active here. Just two days later, on the morning of 26 January, Vernon Austin was carrying out his usual duties as the officer in charge of a gun section. He made sure the gun positions were in order and made his way up through the lanes south of Richebourg up to the Rue de Bois. It was a journey he had made several times, en route to the building he and his fellow gunner officers had selected as an OP. An officer of the 1st KRRC recalled what happened:

> A quiet day and no rain. During the morning 2nd Lieut Austin R.F.A. was killed by a sniper on the road between the headquarters of the Companies in the trenches and the house occupied by the machine guns . . . on our left. We had been warned when we first took over from the Herts that this road was dangerous but we had never had anyone hit walking along it, although it had been used fairly regularly by day as well as by night.[8]

Vernon Austin was killed instantly, by a single shot. From the description here and in other documents it appears the incident took place close to a road junction known to the troops as Chocolate Menier Corner. Chocolate Menier was a famous brand of French chocolate, and a building here had an advertising poster promoting it, hence the name. His battery commander, the third one he had served under since coming to France, wrote home to Sir Herbert Austin:

The ruins of Richebourg church.

Houses on the Rue de Bois at Richebourg, close to Chocolate Menier Corner where Vernon Austin met his death in January 1915.

Your son, who was a Subaltern in my battery, was killed in action this morning about 11.30am. The poor boy and I were alone when he was shot by a sniper. He had accompanied me to a forward position in order to learn the ground, never at any time a very safe business, but necessary. Coming back we had to pass an exposed piece of road. It was at this point that he was shot through the right breast by a rifle bullet, and died within a few minutes without recovering consciousness . . . I need hardly tell you what a gloom it has cast over officers and men of my battery, as everyone was so fond of him . . . He was such a cheery little chap and always showed such a stout front under fire.[9]

The commander of the 34th Brigade, of which 22nd Battery was a part, wrote, 'he was a most keen and capable officer, and his loss is a great loss to the Brigade, with all of whom he was so popular'.[10]

It was a crushing blow to Herbert Austin. In this second year of the war this great patriot had turned his factory over to war work, and now his only son, whom he had planned would follow him into the family business, lay dead on the battlefield. Initially, Vernon was buried at Richebourg, in a field grave close to the Battery site. A wooden cross was placed on his grave, and at this stage in the conflict war graves arrangements were somewhat ad hoc. There were no proper Graves Registration Units and no Imperial (later

Commonwealth) War Graves Commission. With the outcome of the war uncertain, and the future of war graves unknown, many families wished for the graves of their loved ones to be brought home. However, while at this stage the War Office would not prevent such a thing, repatriation was not something it would pay for, especially considering the huge losses in the Army since the outbreak of war.

For Herbert Austin, of course, cost was not an issue. He immediately began to make arrangements for his son's body to be brought home. But where to bury him? Close to the family home was the obvious choice, but both his parents knew of his love of Canterbury and as a master at the school later wrote, 'we are glad to think that his affection for this place was so strong and so constantly expressed, that his father wished him to be buried near his old school'.[11]

Back in France Vernon's comrades of the 22nd Battery exhumed the body, placed it in a coffin and handed it over to a representative of the Austin family, who accompanied it to Boulogne on 6 February 1915, just over ten days after he had been killed. Here it was placed on a ship and taken to Folkestone, where the coffin was met by representatives of a Canterbury Funeral Parlour who brought it into the city in a motorised funeral hearse; quite a rarity in 1915, but fitting given Vernon's background. The nearest burial ground to the school was the churchyard of St Martin's, but first he lay in the Innocent's Chapel in Canterbury Cathedral. Here the coffin was covered in the Union flag, his sword and a wooden cross from his original field grave, which bore the legend 'a last adieu from his comrades on the battlefield'.[12] The family held a private service here, and then the military funeral began; Vernon's coffin was carried on a gun carriage supplied by men of the Royal Horse Artillery through the streets of Canterbury, accompanied by Troopers of the 3rd Cavalry Regiment based at Canterbury's cavalry barracks, and also cadets from the King's School. The cortège arrived at St Martin's where a huge crowd had assembled, which included not only members of the family, but local civil and military representatives and workers from the Austin factory. A volley was fired over his grave and the last post sounded.[13]

Taken from a grave on the Western Front, Vernon Austin was one of only a handful of battlefield casualties who were brought back to England and buried at a place of their families choosing. A few months later the French authorities banned the repatriation of fallen soldiers, and the War Office did likewise. With so many dead, and the war far from over, it would never be possible to repatriate them all, and with so many missing soldiers the War

Vernon Austin's coffin, mounted on a gun carriage, is taken through the streets of Canterbury in February 1915.

Close to Vernon Austin's home, the local village war memorial records his name. (Geoff Sullivan)

Office felt such a system would be unfair to the families of these men. Eventually proper arrangements were made for the burial of the dead and a wartime agreement with the French ensured those buried overseas would lie on ground given in perpetuity. But Vernon James Austin would remain the boy who came home, home to Canterbury where he would lay for all time close to the streets and countryside, and the school, he loved so much.

Researching Vernon James Austin

As the chapters on other officers in this book will explain, generally speaking their records survive better than those of ordinary soldiers. However, for Vernon Austin there is no surviving service record. A different approach was required for researching Austin, but the fact that he had died in the Great War made the work a little easier as his name and details would be recorded in more sources because he had died on the battlefield. The son of a famous father, online he gets quite a few mentions but there is very little about his war and what he did. The starting point, therefore, was an excellent source for officers killed in the first two years of the war – *The Bond of Sacrifice*. This two-volume publication, edited by Colonel L.A. Clutterbuck, who was inspired to work on the project because he had lost a relative in the war, contains photographs and biographies of almost every officer killed in 1914 and many of those killed in 1915. After 1915 the huge number of officer casualties meant it was impossible to continue. While originals of the work are very rare, it has been reprinted by Naval and Military Press, and the 1914 volume was digitised in 2004 by S&N Genealogy Supplies.

This source provided a lot of detail for Vernon Austin, and also a photograph of him. It also made mention of his education and as he had attended King's School in Canterbury, contact was made with them. Like many public schools of the period they published a school magazine and the school's archivist was able to provide copies of articles in it relating to Austin. It is always worth contacting public schools and colleges as they often have detailed records and good photographic collections. The school magazine gave information on the artillery unit he served with, which then lead to a search of the unit War Diary in document class WO95 at TNA. Being an officer, Austin was mentioned in the diary and for the battery he served with there was also a separate diary for 1914 which gave much more detail on their movements. In the month he died the artillery papers mentioned they were supporting another regiment, 1st Battalion King's Royal Rifle Corps, and so their diary was also looked at for some context as to what was happening in the front line. This is always worth doing, and in

Vernon Austin's unique grave at Canterbury.

this case resulted in the bonus of his death being reported and described by the adjutant of this battalion, thus giving more information about the circumstances of his death and also assisting in identifying where it actually happened, as the infantry diary provided more information about place than the artillery one.

Local newspapers were also consulted. These valuable sources of information are normally found in local reference libraries and local study centres. Some county record offices also have them, and many newspapers still exist and may have microfilm copies of back issues. A complete collection is in the National Newspaper Library in Colindale. This source gave more details of his elaborate funeral and led to his grave at Canterbury, which while listed in the Commonwealth War Graves Commission's database, is not the standard headstone; it is a special and unique grave, sited in the grounds of the oldest parish church in England.

Notes

1. The *Cantuarian*, 1915, courtesy of the King's School archives.
2. E. Wyrall, *The History of the Second Division Volume I 1914–1916* (Thomas Nelson & Sons, 1921), p. xiv.
3. 1st Battalion King's Royal Rifle Corps War Diary TNA WO95/1358. Crown Copyright.
4. Wyrall, *The History of the Second Division*, p. 25.
5. Ibid., p. 26.
6. Ibid., p. 50.
7. L.A. Clutterbuck, *The Bond of Sacrifice Volume I* (Anglo-African Publishing, 1915), p. 456.
8. 1st Battalion King's Royal Rifle Corps War Diary TNA WO95/1358. Crown Copyright.
9. The *Cantuarian*, 1915, courtesy of the King's School archives.
10. Ibid.
11. Ibid.
12. Ibid.
13. *Canterbury Times*, 8 February 1915, courtesy of the King's School archives.

Chapter Two

WHERE ARE THE BOYS OF THE VILLAGE TONIGHT?

Roy Fazan and the Wadhurst Tragedy

The 'Pals' battalions of the Great War have become, nearly a century later, almost a part of common folklore when the history of the war is written. The idea of eager volunteers from the same community – men who had grown up together, worked and played together, drank together in the local pubs – all joining up as volunteers on the outbreak of war is something very much associated with the tragic nature of the conflict. Few realise that the idea of 'Pals' units pre-dated the war, and had their roots firmly in the local Territorial battalions. In April 1908 the Territorial Force was created; it would become the Territorial Army after the Great War. Across the country county regiments formed Territorial battalions. The personnel in the Territorial battalions were not full-time soldiers; they could carry on their normal civilian lives, but were required to do regular drill sessions at their local Drill Hall and attend annual camps. In return they would receive payment, and in time of war they would be mobilised and these part-time soldiers could relieve regular battalions on garrison duty and allow them to serve overseas. The formation of the Territorial Force proved largely successful, although few units were at full strength when the war broke out.

In the county of Sussex, three Territorial battalions were formed; the 4th based in West Sussex with a headquarters at Horsham, the 5th (Cinque Ports) in the East based at Hastings and the 6th (Cyclist) in Brighton. In the very rural communities of East Sussex, the 5th Battalion recruited heavily among the many estates and in the small villages. Infantry battalions at this time were broken down into eight companies lettered A to H, and this enabled localised companies to be formed, drawing in men from these specific communities. In the 5th these companies and where they recruited were:

A Company: Hastings
B Company: Battle
C Company: Ticehurst & Wadhurst
D Company: Lewes
E Company: Rye
F Company: Uckfield
G Company: Crowborough
H Company: Ore

C Company had a Drill Hall in Wadhurst, and recruited in the area between Wadhurst and Ticehurst to the east, and small villages like Stonegate to the south. The majority of the men in the company came from Wadhurst, a fairly small Sussex village with a population of just over 3,600 in 1911. The main local employer was the land; it was a community steeped in agriculture, although it had once been at the hub of the Sussex iron industry, but that was in steep decline by the twentieth century. Aside from a collection of small shops and local traders, there was also a local doctor, who was very much at the heart of village life. Charles Herbert Fazan, a

Men of the Wadhurst company on annual camp, 1912.

The Fazan family home and local surgery in the village of Wadhurst as it is today.

Roy Fazan, 1914.

Londoner who had moved to Sussex to practise medicine, had been the local physician for more than twenty-five years by the time the Great War broke out. He had two sons, Eric and Roy, both of whom had grown up in the village until they had gone off to school. Young Roy had been educated at Epsom, and by 1914 both he and his brother were training as medical students in London. Roy was studying at the University of London, and aside from his studies he was also a keen amateur rugby player and member of the Rosslyn Park Rugby Club in Roehampton, where he regularly played.[1] In the early summer of 1914 he decided to follow the example of his elder brother, now married, and he joined the Wadhurst company, being commissioned in the 5th Battalion in May 1914. The company on the eve of the war therefore reflected the whole strata of the community; from the sons of the middle classes like Roy to the lads who tilled the land and bailed the hay in harvest time.

When the war broke out the 5th Battalion was mobilised. It had just completed the annual camp but as an entire battalion it was below strength. The pre-war establishment should have been 29 officers and 982 men,[2] but the actual strength was well under this figure by more than 40 per cent. As with other Territorial battalions in Sussex and across the country, the battalion opened its doors to wartime volunteers in August 1914 and as there were no other units formed here at that time, they were inundated with recruits. The battalion was soon full, but still the men kept coming and so a second, and then a third battalion of the 5th were formed. The original battalion became the 1/5th Battalion Royal Sussex Regiment, with the wartime raised ones known as 2/5th and 3/5th. The new members of the 1/5th were largely drawn from towns like Lewes and Hastings, and so to some extent the 'local' nature of some of the companies was dispersed and the battalion went from eight companies to four, amalgamating the old ones to form:

A (Hastings) & E (Rye) became A Company
B (Battle) & F (Uckfield) became B Company
C (Ticehurst & Wadhurst) & D (Lewes) became C Company
G (Crowborough) & H (Ore) became D Company

Roy Fazan now found himself a platoon commander in C Company, remaining with those he knew from Wadhurst. His brother was posted to A Company, which he would eventually command. A short period of garrison duty in the Tower of London followed, and as 1914 moved into 1915 it was increasingly clear to those in command on the Western Front that Territorial

A world away from what lay ahead; the officers' mess of the 5th Royal Sussex, frequented by the Fazan brothers.

soldiers would now be required on the battlefield. Prior to the war a scheme called the Imperial Service Obligation had been introduced to entice Territorials to agree to overseas service in time of war; under their original conditions they had signed up for home service only. In some battalions the number of men who had agreed to this was higher than in others, and several pre-war commanders had insisted that everyone sign up for it, although it was a voluntary scheme. For whatever reason, the 1/5th Battalion had a very high percentage of men who had signed this agreement, and so was one of the Territorial battalions selected to be sent overseas as soon as possible. Therefore, on 16 February 1915 the battalion was inspected at the Tower of London, and two days later marched to Waterloo station, took the train for Southampton and embarked on SS *Pancras* for Le Havre. Roy Fazan marched at the head of his platoon through the streets of London; he and the Wadhurst boys were now at war.

On arrival in France the battalion spent a couple of days in a rest camp at Le Havre before proceeding via train to the village of Allouagne in Northern France. Here they joined a Brigade of the 1st Division which also contained the 2nd Battalion Royal Sussex Regiment, one of the regular battalions that the 1/5th had often trained with in camp and which several men in the battalion had brothers, cousins or friends serving in. Commanded by Lieutenant Colonel Frederick Langham, the 1/5th felt it a great honour to be serving alongside regular soldiers of the same regiment. During the Battle of Neuve Chapelle on 10 March 1915, Britain's first offensive battle of the war, they were held in reserve in a small village close to the front but their first experience in the trenches was a few days later when they took over positions close to the village of Festubert. Roy and his platoon settled down to a period of static trench warfare, holding fairly primitive positions at Festubert and south of the Rue du Bois at Richebourg l'Avoué. This flat piece of land had a trench system running parallel to the road, the Rue du Bois, with a few old farm tracks pointing out to no-man's-land and the German front line. One of these was called the Cinder Track, as before the war the farm had attempted to make it more passable in the bad weather by covering the path with ash and cinders. Roy's brother Eric later described the positions here, 'there followed tours of duty in the trenches, breastworks, and advanced posts called "grouse butts" in the Bethune area'.[3]

By April 1915 a new weapon had become a feature of the battlefield – gas. Gas was first used on the Western Front by the Germans at Ypres on 22 April 1915. The early gas was chlorine based, released from canisters and relied on the wind to carry it across the battlefield to the enemy beyond. British reaction to the gas was swift and within a few days anti-gas measures were

Lieutenant Colonel Freddy Langham (right), 1914.

put in place and the first early gas masks issued to the men. For Roy and his brother Eric it was now a part of their daily life and by early May their responsibilities as officers now involved ensuring their men were issued with the masks allocated to them – small pads of cotton gauze impregnated with a solution to counteract the effects of the gas. While primitive, it was an advance on the 'Mark I' gas mask that comprised a handkerchief soaked in the soldier's own urine, which men at Ypres had been forced to use.

While the British Army was fighting a bitter defence of Ypres at this time, as the Germans advanced and used gas more and more to assist in a breakthrough, a plan was already in hand to launch a second British offensive on the same front where the Battle of Neuve Chapelle had taken place in March. This became known as the Battle of Aubers Ridge, and while Douglas Haig's First Army hoped to rupture the German line and affect a breakthrough, it was as much an effort to relieve some pressure upon the defenders up in Flanders. The 1st Division, of which Roy Fazan's 1/5th Royal Sussex was a part, was charged with attacking the German lines on the right flank of the Aubers battlefield. Having taken the trenches and redoubts across the plain from their own positions at Richebourg, the next objective would be the rising ground of the Aubers Ridge beyond; the feature that gave the battle its name. The main assault was to involve the regular battalions of the division, and the 1/5th would be in support. Colonel Langham, while anxious to take his men into battle, was probably relieved they were not in the first wave, as there had been a measles outbreak in the 1/5th, and their battle strength was now down to some 600 officers and men. Even Roy Fazan's own platoon had been depleted, and several of his Wadhurst men were in hospital.

The weather broke bright and clear on the morning of 9 May 1915, the day of the attack. The men were in place around Richebourg and the Rue du Bois, with the 1/5th in reserve to the right of the Cinder Track. As soon as the advance started it was clear that failure would be the only outcome as the assaulting waves were met at Zero Hour with murderous machine-gun fire, the barrage having been unable to destroy the German defences. Colonel Langham wrote home to his counterpart in the 2/5th Battalion, describing the events of 9 May:

> Our Brigade had to attack. The assaulting line, 2nd Sussex on the left, and the Northamptons on the right . . . 2nd Line: ourselves on the left, and the 2nd K.R.R. on the right. 3rd Line: 1st Loyal North Lancs on the left and 9th King's Liverpools on the right. Our job was to 'mop up' the trenches after the assaulting line had taken them, and support

our second battalion and the Northants . . . We had therefore to 'mop up' on the front of the two assaulting battalions and it meant sending up a third company to follow the K.R.R's and 'mop up' behind the Northants. After a bombardment of 40 minutes to break up the German barbed wire and smash up the parapet, the advance began. Three companies of the 2nd Battalion and all the Northants were out over and got to from 40 to 80 yards from the German lines. 'C' Coy, less one platoon, 'A' Coy, less one platoon, and the whole of 'B' Coy, went out in the second line . . . Then the most murderous rifle and machine gun and shrapnel fire opened, and no-one could get on or get back. People say the fire at Mons and Ypres was nothing to it. No end of brave things were done, and our men were splendid, but helpless. They simply had to wait to be killed. After some considerable time we got orders to retire, but this was easier said than done. Some men were 300 yards out from our parapet, many dead, and some even on fire, and in two cases men of ours who were burning alive, committed suicide, one by blowing out his own brains, and another cut his own jugular vein with the point of his bayonet. Every now and again you would see men roll over on the ground. Then men began to crawl in, most of them wounded.[4]

Langham found that some men had actually stayed out on the battlefield,

Lieutenant Colonel Freddy Langham with headquarters staff at the Tower of London, 1914.

and when the next phase of the attack went in:

> The Black Watch and 1st Camerons then assaulted and got it just as badly as we did: though a few got in, only to be bayoneted. Several of our men, still alive, got up and joined them in their charge, after lying out there 12 hours! Unfortunately I cannot find that any of these brave fellows got back safe, though there may be some among the wounded.[5]

He estimated that casualties were well above 200 officers and men, which accounted for a very high percentage of the 2 companies involved. He had to conclude sadly that the missing were most likely among the dead, as the chances of men being taken prisoner were slim under the circumstances. Later he was to estimate that those who went over into no-man's-land suffered at least 77 per cent casualties. As they came out he recalled:

The Pelham brothers, both from Wadhurst, who died in the fighting on 9 May 1915.

> at six o'clock the regiment was ordered to march away to Le Touret, where they would be told their destination by the Staff. The remnants of the battalion were formed up, numbered off, and marched away in fours, singing 'Sussex By The Sea' as they went down the road, in spite of the drubbing we had received in the morning.[6]

Once back in billets the work began on assessing the full cost of the battle. Langham's figures proved pretty accurate and he was sadly correct on the missing; none of them ever turned up and they were eventually officially reported as having been killed in action. The worst losses, Langham found, were in B Company commanded by Captain G.L. Courthope, the son of a major local land owner at Wadhurst. Within a few hours Courthope was snowed under with writing letters to the next of kin of men from his company killed and wounded. He immediately noticed an alarming trend: one place had been affected greatly, his own village of Wadhurst. He quickly wrote to the local village priest:

You have doubtless heard we have been in a big fight and lost heavily. My poor company lost four officers and 102 NCOs and men in the assault out of 154 whom I took into action. They covered themselves with glory. Will you and other kind friends help me to notify the families? I am overwhelmed with work, and can for the moment do no more than send the list of casualties . . . which nominally comes from your parish.[7]

Back in the parish one of the first signs that something was amiss came from a wounded survivor of the attack who lived in the village, Private William Skinner.

We are back from one of the biggest bombardments known, and it is a wonder I am alive to tell the tale . . . I am the only one left out of nine in [my] Section . . . All the others are either killed, missing or wounded. Captain Courthope is safe but Lieut Fazan is killed . . . It was something awful. About 6.30 in the morning we were in reserve to the 2nd Sussex Regiment. We tried to capture the trenches, but as soon as we leaped over the trench the enemy had machineguns trained on us. We had to lie down. I partially buried myself by using my bayonet and one round of ammunition. I had to stay there from 6.30 in the morning until 8.30 in the evening. It was terrible . . . One bullet went through my haversack, and another through my waterproof sheet . . . I cannot bear to think of it.[8]

The news arrived at the Fazan home a few days after the attack. There was a letter from Eric saying he was safe but with the terrible news about young Roy, and an official telegram from the War Office. Dr Fazan and his wife were thrown in mourning, but they were far from alone. Talk of the big battle rang throughout the village, as it soon became apparent that twenty-one men from the Wadhurst company had been killed and at least twice that number wounded. For a village the size of Wadhurst the loss of twenty-one men in one day was catastrophic, but these weren't the only casualties from 9 May 1915. In addition, two other men serving with the 2nd Battalion as regulars had been killed, and the schoolmaster's son had died serving as an officer in another regiment. Company Sergeant Major Albert Freeland had been wounded in the eye in the attack. An old soldier aged 45, he died of these wounds a few weeks later making the total deaths related to that one day a staggering twenty-five. Eric Fazan later concluded:

in a Territorial unit, because it is recruited locally, casualties even in a platoon can grievously affect some town or hamlet at home. Thus it

A modern view looking down the Cinder Track from the German positions, showing the direction of the attack on 9 May 1915.

was that on that tragic Sunday several villages in East Sussex were plunged suddenly into mourning – in the parish church of one alone are on record the names of 21 of the 5th Royal Sussex as killed in action on that day. And that is the reason why a parade and service of remembrance of 'May the 9th' has been held each year ever since.[9]

These losses are largely unknown outside of Sussex, while the tremendous losses on the Somme involving Northern Pals battalions on 1 July 1916 have become part of popular history. But when that figure of 25 men is measured against the population of the village, and the 649 men listed on the village's Roll of Honour, it shows that, quite probably, Wadhurst suffered proportionally the heaviest casualties in a single community anywhere in England during the Great War for one day's battle. While lost on the outside world, the echoes of the fallen would remain in Wadhurst for many years. In the 1920s a war memorial was placed in the local church. Unusually, and to emphasise the effect of 9 May on the village, the names were listed in date order. Standing there it is quite apparent how dominant that one day is. The memorial also helped the families of the Aubers Ridge dead to reach what is now called 'closure' – of the men who died that day only two have known graves. The bodies of Roy Fazan and the majority of the 1/5th Battalion men were never found, and while their names were later engraved on the Le Touret Memorial close to where they fell, the families of missing soldiers were arguably tortured in a way that those with graves to visit, and means of accepting their loss, were not.

The Fazan family gradually came to terms with their own loss, and Charles Fazan continued as the local doctor. For the rest of his working life he would meet the families of those who had died with his son Roy, and one wonders what conversations were held in addition to discussing personal ailments, especially around the anniversary of 9 May. His elder son Eric eventually succeeded him as the local GP, and by the time he retired the local doctor in Wadhurst had been a Fazan for more than seventy-five years. Eric named one of his sons Roy in memory of his brother, something his father very much approved of. The memory of the young man who had so

That deathly day shown in stark reality through the chronologically listed names on the Wadhurst War Memorial.

Eric Fazan's grave in Wadhurst churchyard showing the memorial to his son, Roy, named after his brother, and who died in Normandy in 1944.

wanted to be a doctor lived on, but in a strange case of symmetry the second Roy Fazan went to war in 1939, once more with the county regiment, the Royal Sussex. He served in the Middle East, became an Army Commando and was killed in action in Normandy on 7 June 1944. Two doctors' sons, two Roy Fazans – one who fell in the Great War, and one in the Second World War. The sufferings of a small Sussex village went on and deaths like these added even great poignancy to the popular song, 'where are the boys of the village tonight?'

Researching Roy Fazan and the Wadhurst Company

Although this is the story of the Fazans, and especially Roy Fazan who died at Aubers Ridge, it covers a wider aspect of looking at an entire unit recruited in a specific location. Local research like this can be greatly assisted by a visit to a county record office and local newspaper offices. With the research on Fazan and the Wadhurst men local newspapers for the area were found in the East Sussex Record Office in Lewes on microfilm, although they could also be consulted in their original form at the National Newspaper Library at Colindale, London. These papers provided a great deal of information about local men from the Wadhurst company, and featured extracts from their letters. Following the casualties at Aubers Ridge the same papers also contained obituaries and details of the wounded, making it possible to build up a great deal of background on the men involved in the battle. The same type of research can be used for any locality, especially in the early war period of 1914–15 when the censorship of local newspapers was almost non-existent and they published a great deal of information on men who survived and local units.

The battalion's War Diary in WO95 at TNA provided evidence of the day-to-day activities when overseas, and some added detail was found in Eric Fazan's history of the battalion he wrote during his retirement. The Royal Sussex Regiment is unusual in that it has exceptionally good regimental archives; most regiments lost or destroyed theirs during the many years of regimental amalgamation following the Second World War. The regiment has a museum in Eastbourne, and this should always be the first place to contact when enquiring about any regiment's archives, but in this case – as with many – the actual records are now in the care of the West Sussex Record Office in Chichester, the city that was once the home of the regimental depot. The collection here is so vast that a catalogue of it was published, and there are plans to put details of what is available on the

Internet. Such archives can be consulted in person, but they often offer a research service for a small fee.

Researching a localised battalion also means making some enquiries in that locality itself, as very often there are many visual reminders of past connections. In the small village of Wadhurst the terrific losses at Aubers Ridge are brought home through the war memorial in the church where the casualties are listed in date order, and the dominance of 9 May 1915 is clearly visible. The old Drill Hall used by the Wadhurst company was demolished, but the Fazans' house was found, although it is now divided into flats. A research visit and interviewing some of the locals also resulted in finding the Fazan family grave and discovering that a local road has been named in their honour. While such research is often possible via the Internet, nothing really substitutes for good fieldwork which can often uncover useful information not available elsewhere.

Notes

1. This rugby club created a memorial to its former members who died in the war, and has a fine website that includes details of Roy Fazan at: www. rugbyremembers.co.uk; accessed 1 March 2010.
2. Details compiled from War Office establishments, October 1913.
3. E.A.C. Fazan, *Cinque Ports Battalion* (Sussex, 1971), p. 105.
4. Personal account by Lieutenant Colonel F.G. Langham from papers in the West Sussex Record Office.
5. Ibid.
6. Ibid.
7. *Sussex Express*, 21 May 1915.
8. Ibid.
9. Fazan, *Cinque Ports Battalion*, pp. 108–9.

Chapter Three

BRITAIN'S SEA SOLDIERS AT GALLIPOLI

Frederick James Stoneham

In the years before the Great War there was a developing tradition of part-time service in the armed forces of Great Britain. The need for this was related to the worsening international situation combined with the fear that Britain's small regular forces would be inadequate in time of war; Britain was the only major power that did not rely on universal conscription to build its armed forces. The role and development of Territorial Force (later Territorial Army) units of the Army, which succeeded generations of service of Volunteer units is well known. However, the role of Volunteers in naval units is largely forgotten. Yet across the country in the years before the Great War localised units of the Royal Naval Volunteer Reserve (RNVR) were formed so that men with naval skills and experience could be trained to a given standard and called on in time of conflict, but at the same time their commitment was only part-time and they were free to follow their chosen civilian career. These so-called 'Divisions' were naturally focused on some of the big ports or cities with a tradition of seafaring connections, such as Bristol, Clydeside and Liverpool. Sussex also formed a Division, based around the many numerous seaside towns that littered the Sussex shoreline: Brighton, Eastbourne, Hastings Rye and Worthing are just a handful of examples of towns that supplied men to the Sussex RNVR.

The town of Eastbourne had a strong Sussex RNVR contingent prior to 1914, based around the local fisherman. Fishing as an industry in

FORGET ME NOT.

Fred Stoneham not long after joining the Royal Naval Division in 1914.

Eastbourne went back to Roman times, but the attraction of service in the RNVR was not just limited to those whose trade was at sea. Frederick James Stoneham was a young 17-year-old mechanic at the local bus company in Eastbourne, working for the Corporation Motor Bus department. His parents ran the Dining Room at the Colonnades, close to the seafront in an area popular with Edwardian holiday-makers. It is likely that his engineering skills are what got him into the unit, although a young man growing up close to the sea probably spent some time in boats if service in a naval unit attracted him in later life. Fred, as the family called him, joined on 23 July 1914, just under two weeks before the outbreak of war, and at a time when Europe was gradually falling into chaos following the assassination of the heir to the Austrian throne in Sarajevo the month before. Indeed, such news would have filled the local newspapers and it is possibly one of the reasons that prompted him to enlist. Service in a military unit in his town was not an option at that time, as there was no local Drill Hall and no Eastbourne company of the local Territorial battalion, the 5th (Cinque Ports) Royal Sussex Regiment. His enlistment papers show him to have been 5ft 7in tall, with a fair complexion, brown hair and blue eyes.

Events moved on at a pace probably not anticipated by Fred Stoneham that summer. He found himself mobilised on 2 August, with orders to report to the local headquarters. When Britain declared war on the 4th he and the men of the Eastbourne contingent were told to report to the Sussex RNVR Headquarters at Hove. Here the men from the county were assembled in the substantial Drill Hall prior to being posted to Crystal Palace. The majority of them had joined the RNVR thinking that it would mean service at sea in time of war, and were no doubt a little confused with the posting to London, but unbeknown to them they were about to form part of a formation unique to the First World War, the Royal Naval Division.

The origins of the Royal Naval Division were in the creation of an 'Advanced Base Force' for the Admiralty prior to 1914. This force consisted of Royal Marine Light Infantry units formed from their various Divisions and could be used as a land force in time of a European conflict. Once the war broke out, and this force found itself committed to service in Ostend a few weeks later, it was realised it would be inadequate and that some type of proper formation would be required. Pioneered by Winston Churchill, then Lord of the Admiralty, two Naval Brigades were formed from personnel in the RNVR. There were eight 'Battalions' created, each one named after a famous admiral: Drake, Hawke, Benbow, Collingwood, Nelson, Howe, Hood and Anson. Each battalion comprised 937 naval officers and men, and once formed were mobilised for service to support the Royal Marines in Belgium. For some reason, possibly due to his age, Fred Stoneham did not go to Antwerp with the Howe Battalion he had been posted to. Instead, he was posted back to Crystal Palace, which had now become the Depot of the Royal Naval Division. Here he would remain until the RNVR units returned from Flanders, and the whole division now concentrated at Blandford Camp in Dorset. The experience in Europe had shown that there were many shortcomings in the Division; naval officers had had difficulty with land navigation, and 3 units had unwittingly crossed the border into Holland and been interned, resulting in more than 1,500 officers and men being prisoners for the remainder of the war. These 'lost' battalions had to be reconstituted and proper training for future operations implemented for new recruits and those like Fred who had not seen service overseas. This new start also saw a new unit for Fred, as he was now posted to the Nelson Battalion, named after the most famous military figure in British history, Lord Nelson of Trafalgar. But would Fred and the Royal Naval Division ever be committed to battle again after the experience of 1914?

With the entry of Ottoman Empire, now modern Turkey, into the war in October 1914 on the side of the Central Powers led by Germany, a situation arose where Britain's ally, Russia, could not be re-enforced in the Black Sea from the Aegean Sea and Mediterranean as the Ottomans blocked the Dardanelles, making the passage of ships impossible. It was clear this situation could not continue, and in November 1914 Churchill put forward a bold plan for a naval operation to end the blockade. The War Office was reluctant to commit any troops or resources to this initial plan, and the Royal Naval Division found itself en route to the Aegean Sea as part of the

Men from the Royal Naval Division in training in Dorset prior to sailing for Gallipoli.

Mediterranean Expeditionary Force. Naval operations in the area in February 1915 were inconclusive and a full-scale naval attack on 18 March resulted in disaster with several British and French ships being sunk. Breaking the blockade by a naval attack along a coast with good defences was clearly impossible, and the idea of a landing then came into being. This would require ground troops, and while the Royal Naval Division was close at hand, more than one formation would be needed. Reluctantly, the War Office allocated further British, Australian and New Zealand troops from Egypt, and a fleet set sail to land men on the Gallipoli peninsula at the entrance to the Dardanelles.

Fred Stoneham and his comrades in the Nelson Battalion had been training and re-equipping in Egypt. The blue naval uniforms they had worn at Blandford were exchanged for khaki drill tunics and Wolseley sun helmets. Contemporary photographs show they were equipped with the older pattern 'Long' Lee–Enfield rifles, and surprisingly no aspect of their training had dealt with seaborne landings. The assumption was they would simply arrive at Gallipoli in rowing boats from transport ships, row ashore and advance on Istanbul. Here the troops would besiege the Ottomans and force a surrender. On board SS *Minnetonka*, the Nelson Battalion had pulled out of the island base of Mudros and headed for Gallipoli. As the landings began on 25 April 1915 with Australians and New Zealanders (ANZAC) on one beachhead, and British troops at Cape Helles, they were not initially committed. At this stage in the campaign the Royal Naval Division was not fighting as a coherent formation, and was split up among the various beaches. Fred and the Nelson Battalion were attached to the Australians, and not brought ashore until 29 April. No doubt keen for the fight, the men instead found themselves working on dugouts as April passed into May. The landings had gone badly, the Turks put up much more resistance than anticipated, and now Gallipoli was rapidly turning into a microcosm of the

Home on leave in Eastbourne before he went to Gallipoli, Fred Stoneham (bottom left) had his photograph taken with some of his comrades.

Western Front: trenches and dugouts were now the objectives, and all talks of an advance on Istanbul had diminished.

At ANZAC – the beach area where the Australians and New Zealanders had landed and that was now named after their formation title – the Nelson Battalion settled into a support role. The infrastructure here quickly developed. The Australians had advanced to the high ground beyond the beach in the first few days. There had been no link up with the British at Cape Helles, and the Turks had contained them on the high ground. It was stalemate for now, and as the distance from the beach to the front line was not much more than a mile, no proper rest area existed, and gradually casualties mounted as shells rained down, and men succumbed to sickness. This was always a great problem at Gallipoli as supplies of clean water were non-existent to start with and had to be shipped in. Food soon became tainted with flies, and disease spread. Although eager to take part in operations rather than just act as a labourer, Fred got some idea of the chaos at Gallipoli when he was sent with men from his battalion to support a joint Australian–New Zealand attack on the night of 2/3 May 1915, only to find: 'the New Zealanders not in evidence, and no one having any knowledge of their whereabouts (they were actually digging in a quarter of a mile further to the left) . . . [therefore] the Nelson companies remained, accordingly, till dawn fruitlessly digging in with entrenching tools in the rear of the thinly held Australian line'.[1] But this inactivity wouldn't last for long. Orders arrived to attack in a flanking movement around the 13th Battalion Australian Imperial Force (AIF) ahead of them.

> The Nelson companies had failed to drive home their flanking attack directed against an advanced machine gun position, and were ordered by the Australian Commander to retire. Unfortunately . . . the terrors of the night battle had led to a good deal of disorganisation . . . and something in the nature of a temporary panic broke out. The position was, however, restored, and the Nelson companies rallied in a gully . . . Here from 6am till dusk a memorable stand was made. By the afternoon . . . it became clear that it was only a useless waste of life to cling on in the centre to a position which could not possibly be held against a determined assault such as its importance to the enemy would certainly produce. But before the position could be surrendered, countless wounded, and stores and ammunition had to be cleared. Under constant harassing from the enemy this was successfully achieved, and at 5.30 the garrison were able to begin an exceedingly cool and well planned retreat.[2]

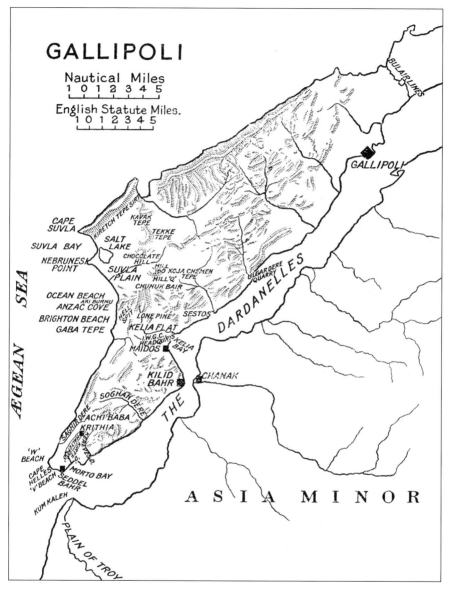

GALLIPOLI

Nautical Miles
1 0 1 2 3 4 5

English Statute Miles.
1 0 1 2 3 4 5

BULAIR LINES

GALLIPOLI

CAPE SUVLA

KIRETCH TEPE SIRT

KAVAK TEPE

TEKKE TEPE

SUVLA BAY

SALT LAKE

NEBRUNESI POINT

CHOCOLATE HILL

HILL 60 KOJA CHEMEN TEPE

HILL 'Q'

ULGARDERE QUARRY

SUVLA PLAIN

CHUNUK BAIR

OCEAN BEACH

ARI BURNU

ANZAC COVE

HELL SPIT

LONE PINE

SESTOS

BRIGHTON BEACH

GABA TEPE

KELIA FLAT

I.W.G.C. HEADQUR'S

KELIA BAY

MAIDOS

KILID BAHR

CHANAK

SOGHAN DERE

ACHI BABA

SAGHIR DERE

KRITHIA

'W' BEACH

CAPE HELLES

'V' BEACH

MORTO BAY

SEDDEL BAHR

KUM KALEH

AEGEAN SEA

DARDANELLES

THE

ASIA MINOR

PLAIN OF TROY

Map of the Gallipoli battlefields, 1915.

Fred had by some miracle survived, but in its first taste of combat at Gallipoli the Nelson Battalion had lost over 200 officers and men, including 3 senior officers. They had little to show for it, and their historian later had to conclude 'the local results of this costly and unfortunate affair were intangible'.[3]

After this they were in support again and now held trenches on the extreme left flank of the positions at ANZAC. From here Fred and his comrades could look out across the Aegean Sea, and north to the flat salt lake of Suvla Bay, which would feature later in the campaign. But,

> the trenches on the extreme left held by the Nelson Battalion backed on to a sandy gorge opening out to the sea. The sides of the cliffs were precipitous, and cut by the wind and rain of the unequal climate into sharp edges, bare of all vegetation; only birds and insects seemed to abound, and at one and the same time could be seen vultures, pigeons, shrikes, martins, swallows and small greyish hawks, while the trenches abounded in yellow centipedes, caterpillars, lizards, and brown and blue butterflies.[4]

In this strange landscape they remained, in a state of inactivity, until they were relieved and moved by boat to Cape Helles. The Royal Naval Division was now reforming as a complete formation and as May went into June, plans for a new attack to break the stalemate at Helles would involve Fred and the men of the Nelson Battalion.

As at ANZAC, the landings at Cape Helles had been successful on the first day of the campaign, but the British troops had barely got much beyond them. They were stuck in a flat plateau cut by gullies or nullahs, with the Turks holding high ground beyond and with a system of trenches around a small village called Krithia. A comrade of Fred's, James Hart, described the scene:

> After a time I began to wonder where the British, and French were holding their position. Away in the front of me, about six miles was a huge hill running right across the peninsular and appeared to me like another Gibraltar, an impregnable position, held by the enemy. This hill is known as Achi Baba and stands at a height of 860 feet above the sea level, giving the enemy full survey of the land in front. Knowing every inch of the ground we had taken from them, they could drop shells wherever it was their wish. The nature of the country was very rugged, and proved a difficult task for our troops, as the land to them was strange. This was the hill we were trying to wrest from the Turks.

In the trenches at Krithia, June 1915.

> On my left I could see the remains of what was once a Turkish village namely Korithia [*sic*]. It had been smashed to pieces in the first bombardment of our battleships. All that remains of it are a few ruined walls.[5]

Several attacks to dislodge the Turkish defenders in May had failed, and a major attempt to advance the line forward was planned for 4 June. A total of three divisions would attack simultaneously, with the Royal Naval Division on the right, close to the French troops who shared this part of the battlefield. During a critical moment in this battle the Nelson Battalion was called forward to fill a gap in the line. Losses in other units of the division, and the neighbouring Manchester Regiment battalions, meant they were the only formation of any strength to fill the gap: 'This gap had to be filled, or the last of the morning's gains had to be surrendered . . . the Nelson Battalion were sent forward to get their first experience of active operations south of Achibaba.'[6] But it wasn't an attack at the point of the bayonet that lay ahead, instead they found themselves doing more digging. Their commander came up with a good plan to save the situation here by constructing a new line for the division to occupy, rather than try and hold on to partially captured Turkish trenches ahead. It would mean loss of some ground, but not all of it. Much work was done under darkness, and as daybreak came murderous fire fell down on Fred and his comrades

Resting in a reserve trench at Krithia, June 1915.

labouring in the June sunshine. But the ability to build some protection under darkness meant that cover was available and the task was completed, allowing the shattered survivors of the main attack to pull back to the new line. This successful operation had only cost a handful of casualties, but it did include four dead officers; and this was testimony to the fact that these young commanders had to stand in the open and direct the work of their men.

The heat, the experience of battle and the conditions at Gallipoli were gradually getting to Fred. He was still only 18 years old, and although far from the youngest on the battlefield,[7] the smell of the unburied dead and the fear of those operations in the night around Krithia must have had a profound effect on him. Furthermore, the poor food and water made every man on the Peninsula physically weaker than their counterparts on the Western Front, and with all the labouring tasks the Nelson Battalion had been required to do, somehow it had affected Fred. He was admitted to a Field Ambulance with neuralgia just after the operations at Krithia, and although this nerve-damage-related condition, which causes chronic pain to the sufferer, is difficult to diagnose and was seen by some doctors as 'malingering', it was recognised by the medical officer Fred saw and he was sent to Mudros for treatment. The attack must have been serious, as it kept him in hospital at Mudros for several weeks, and he finally rejoined his unit in the trenches near Krithia on 6 July.

When he returned to the Nelson Battalion, preparations for another offensive were visibly in hand. The Battle of Krithia in June had not gone quite to plan, and the Turks still held the village and high ground beyond, and the line had not advanced further than the trenches Fred had helped dig. The next attempt to break that line was on 12 July 1915, and this time the Royal Naval Division was there in support of the 52nd (Lowland) Division. This Scottish Territorial Division had only been at Gallipoli a few weeks, but this was their second time in action at Krithia. Fred and his comrades spent an anxious time on the 12th listening to the sights and sounds of battle from a position called Backhouse Post. Unbeknown to them, it had gone badly with heavy losses, although they likely had an indication of this as the steady stream of wounded were evacuated past them. This fact was also seemingly not known to the commander in chief at Gallipoli, Sir Iain Hamilton, who ordered the next day that 'three battalions of the Royal Naval Division should reinforce a fresh attack to be made that afternoon, 13th July, on such portions of our original objectives as remained in the enemy's hands. This second attack was a success . . . the Nelson Battalion, on the left of the Royal Naval Division attack, valiantly advanced and made good'.[8]

Those who took part in the battle would have struggled to use the word 'success' in describing it. The historian of the Lowland Division angrily denounced Hamilton's words, and described what he saw as 'a disaster'. The Naval Division historian agreed.

> The losses in the Nelson and Portsmouth Battalions had . . . been disastrous. Lieutenant Colonel Eveleigh and Lieutenant Colonel Luard and ten other officers had been killed. Five other officers and 273 other ranks had become casualties in the Nelson Battalion . . . For the survivors, moreover, clinging desperately to their gains as night came on, the conditions were well-nigh unendurable. Some of the worst scenes ever experienced on the battlefields . . . were crowded into this narrow front of half a mile . . . where many hundreds of men lay dead or dying, where a burning sun had the bodies of the slain to a premature corruption, where there was no resting-place free from physical contamination, where the air, the surface of the ground, and the soil beneath the surface were alike poisonous, fetid, corrupt.[9]

So what had happened? And what of Fred Stoneham? The Nelson Battalion had moved up following orders, to continue with the attack. A long nullah was on their left and their route took them up through a trench they had helped to dig, Nelson Avenue, named after them. From here the fighting

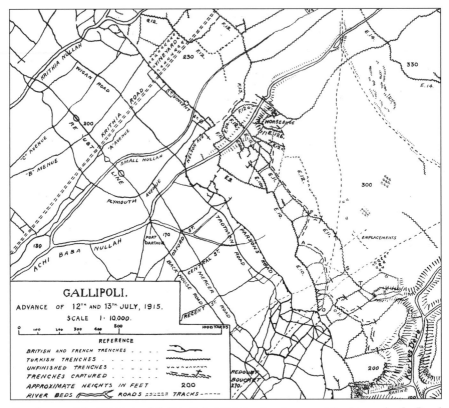

Trench map of the Krithia battlefield in July 1915 showing the ground fought over by the Royal Naval Division.

revolved around trenches in Turkish hands known as the 'F' trenches. One man who was there and left an account of it was James Hart.

About 4.30 pm an order came along the line to be prepared at any time, to move off, and we thought that we were done for the day, and going back to our resting base. But no, we were going back to the front firing line, and when we got there the shells were bursting in the trenches, and upset us a bit. Then an order came down, to fix bayonets, and over the parapet, when the whistle blew, followed by another order, to go over two trenches, and hold on to the third at any cost.

I turned to an old chum of mine, and said 'It's come at last', and shaking hands, and wishing each other the best of good luck, over into the open we went, many of the poor fellows only just got out the trench, and before they had a chance to run were, either killed or badly wounded. I cannot say how it was I missed such a fate, but I simply kept running, and I certainly was not in my right senses. I came to the first trench without getting hit, and beheld a terrible sight. All I could see was dead bodies, and I could hear the dying calling for water, but all I had in my head was to get over two trenches, and hold the third at any cost.

Still running, I came to the second trench, which I believe was a dummy trench, set with mines, so I jumped quite clear of that, and proceeded to the hoped for position. The time I had been running made me begin to feel puffed out, and I began to think that if I went on much longer, at this rate I should soon be on Achi Baba, when all of a sudden I came to a very deep slope in the ground, over which I had to jump. While jumping this little gulf I badly sprained my ankle, and when I got up to make another run for the desired trench I found I could only walk, running was quite out of the question. So I started to walk on again, forgetting the dangers, from the Turkish artillery, machine guns, and rifles . . . All of a sudden a bullet caught me, and it was a very funny sensation for it seemed to twist me round, and then I dropped flat to earth.[10]

Hart was one of the nearly 300 casualties in the battalion, and so was Fred Stoneham. What exactly happened to him was never known; no one survived to describe his last moments under the summer skies. His parents back home in Eastbourne got the fateful telegram just over two weeks later, and with no news save that he was 'missing', put an advertisement in the *Eastbourne Gazette* on 4 August, just over a year after Fred had been mobilised: 'The deepest sympathy is expressed for the bereaved parents. Mr and Mrs Stoneham are anxious to hear from any of the deceased comrades who are in a position to give any information concerning their son.'[11] The news never came, as many Sussex lads serving with the battalion died that day, and not a single survivor ever emerged to be able to tell of Fred's last moments. He remained missing, and his body was never found. Eventually the Admiralty declared him a fatality, and his service papers were stamped 'DD' – Discharged Dead. The attack he died in proved one of the last major engagements at Helles, and the static trench warfare that followed gave way to evacuation in January 1916. Churchill's bold plan had resulted in disaster.

The British returned to Gallipoli in 1919, and again in the early 1920s. The Ottoman Empire had been defeated in Mesopotamia and Palestine in 1918,

The aftermath of the Gallipoli campaign: bones recovered from the battlefields in 1919.

and was in collapse. Allied occupation of the Dardanelles followed for several years, and it gave the British a chance to clear the Gallipoli battlefields and establish permanent cemeteries. Some had been made

A provisional cemetery being worked on and attended by British troops in 1920. Most men, like Fred Stoneham, were never be found.

during the war, but on the return most had been dug up and desecrated. One account stated: 'no wooden crosses remained to mark the graves; though a few unshaped rocks with names engraved thereon were still in place. The crosses had long since been put to baser uses by the inhabitants. Three years had been more than enough to reduce all human remains to clean whitened bones.'[12]

Searches of the ground were made, and in the area around Krithia where Fred had died many hundreds, if not thousands of bodies were found. But very few of them had any identification. In 1915 British servicemen only had one identity disk which was normally removed at the time of death, or which could easily become lost or separated from the body. The chances of Fred's remains ever being found or identified were virtually nil. But the Imperial War Graves Commission already had plans to build a memorial at Gallipoli to those who had no known grave. Designed by Sir John Burnett and completed in 1924, the memorial,

> is both the memorial to the Gallipoli Campaign and to the 20,763 men who fell in that campaign and whose graves are unknown or who were lost or buried at sea in Gallipoli waters. Inscribed on it are the names of all the ships that took part in the campaign and the titles of the army formations and units which served on the Peninsula together with the names of 18,985 sailors, soldiers and marines from the United Kingdom, 248 soldiers from Australia, and 1,530 soldiers of the Indian Army.[13]

Of these 20,000 names more than 750 of them are those of Britain's sea soldiers of the Royal Naval Volunteer Reserve. On Panel 14 is Fred Stoneham, the motor mechanic from Eastbourne with a love of the sea, whose name looks out across the tragic battlefields of 1915 where he and so many of his comrades died.

Researching Frederick James Stoneham

Although the men of the Royal Naval Division were in what was essentially an Army formation and served as soldiers, they were paid by and their records were maintained by the Admiralty. The starting point for men who served in the Royal Naval Division is the digitised service records available on TNA's Documents Online site. Here you can search with just a name and download the record. The original of these were record cards which contained a summary of the man's service, showing his personal details, including when and where he was born, his religion and a physical

The Helles Memorial, which commemorates Fred Stoneham and hundreds of those who died in July 1915.

description of him. The cards also show when he enlisted, which units he was attached to and details of any wounds and transfers, and if he was killed and when. It is not unusual to not find someone in these records as they do not appear to be complete. There are also records of RND service personnel which TNA did not take. These are held in the Army Air Museum at Yeovil, where applications for copies of them can be made.

Operational records kept by the Royal Naval Division took the same form of those in the Army. War Diaries were compiled, although in the 1914 and 1915 the keeping of them was somewhat ad hoc. A number of diaries are found in class ADM137 at TNA, but there are also diaries in WO95. The diaries show the day-to-day activities of the various units, and it is also worth checking some of the Brigade and Divisional headquarters' diaries if you are interested in a specific date or period, as these often include additional battle reports and maps.

Men who served in the Royal Naval Division are not found on the Medal Index Cards unless they were later commissioned in the British Army. Instead they are on the Navy Medal Rolls in ADM171 at TNA. These were huge bound ledgers, but for ease of access they were transferred to microfilm and they will be digitised and available online sometime in 2010/11. They show the basic details about the sailor, what medals he was awarded and who the medals were sent to. Various abbreviations are used in the rolls and TNA website has a guide to the common ones.

The official history of the Royal Naval Division by Douglas Jerrold was originally published in 1927, but has now been reprinted by Naval and Military Press. Several units in the division published their own histories, and these have also been reprinted, and in recent years Pen & Sword books have published histories of the Benbow and Hood battalions. These help to add detail to the war diaries and often include photographs, many of them named. Online Kyle Tallet's website pages about the Royal Naval Division at: www.royalnavaldivision.co.uk are a good starting point, but the number of sites about the division is growing.

The Gallipoli campaign in which Fred Stoneham died has attracted the interest of historians for more than ninety years, but a good general account is Peter Hart and Nigel Steel's *Defeat at Gallipoli*. The *Official History* of the Gallipoli campaign, published in two volumes with maps, is more detailed, and was reprinted by Battery Press and the Imperial War Museum. Maps of the campaign are available on CD-ROM from Naval and Military Press, and a good general guidebook is Major and Mrs Holt's *Gallipoli Battlefields*, and comes with a useful full-colour map.

Notes

1. D. Jerrold, *The Royal Naval Division* (Hutchinson, 1927), p. 121.
2. Ibid., pp. 122–3.
3. Ibid., p. 123.
4. Ibid., pp. 125–6.
5. J.R.J. Hart, *My Part in the Great War*, published online at: www.rayhart.plus.com; accessed 1 March 2010.
6. Jerrold, *The Royal Naval Division*, p. 136.
7. At Skew Bridge Cemetery is the grave of Drummer Joseph Townsend, 1/4th East Lancs, who died on 18 May 1915, aged 15.
8. R.R. Thompson, *The Fifty-Second (Lowland) Division 1914–1918* (Maclehose, Jackson & Co., 1923), p. 122.
9. Jerrold, *The Royal Naval Division*, pp. 145–6.
10. Hart, *My Part in the Great War*.
11. *Eastbourne Gazette*, 4 August 1915.
12. T.J. Pemberton, *Gallipoli To-Day* (Ernest Benn, 1926), p. 40.
13. Anon., *Introduction to Helles Memorial Register* (Imperial War Graves Commission, *c*. 1928), p. 10.

Chapter Four

ALL QUIET ON THE WESTERN FRONT – A GREEK PRINTER IN THE TRENCHES

Alexis Ectos Maffuniades

The history of the Great War is often written in terms of big battles and major engagements: Ypres, the Somme and Passchendaele have all become bywords for the sacrifice on the Western Front. The reality of the war was that operations like these only occupied a minority of a soldier's time. Most of his experience in the trenches was in a location somewhere along the hundred or so miles of the Western Front held by the British Expeditionary Force, just holding the line. No big battle, no attack, no battle honour. Such places were referred to as 'quiet sectors' but again the reality was that they were anything but. Each day a soldier was in the front line with his battalion there would be shell fire; artillery shells dropping on a regular basis, fire from enemy trench mortars, and as the war progressed hand grenades and then rifle grenades were used, and gas became a regular feature used often on a daily basis. Add to this work on the barbed wire in front of the trenches, putting men in an exposed position even at night, patrols into no-man's-land, the ground between both sides' front lines, enemy sniper activity and tunnelling, where both sides tunnelled under the battlefield to place charges of explosive at key points, then there was hardly a part of the British front that ever was truly 'quiet'. The outcome of all this activity

Formed in London in September 1914, the 'Stockbrokers' Battalion' of the Royal Fusiliers moved to Colchester, where they are seen marching through the streets. Not every man had a rifle at this stage.

was that the majority of soldiers went to war and experienced this sort of conflict; not bayonets fixed and Over the Top, but the deadlock of attritional trench warfare. And the majority of men who died in the war did not die in the famous battles, but insignificant corners of Northern France and Belgium, just doing their 'bit'.

Alexis Ectos Maffuniades was a member of London's growing Edwardian Greek community. His father had been born in Constantinople (now Istanbul) in 1847, in the heart of Turkey. There had always been a sizeable Greek community there but under the rule of the Ottoman Empire the Greeks had been persecuted. Many left, and London was one place they headed for as there had been a history of Greek immigration in the city since the seventeenth century. Ectos' father was a master litho-printer and it was this business he established in Tottenham, in several locations just off Tottenham High Road. He married in 1889 and had six children, of which Ectos was the youngest. Educated at Tottenham Grammar School, Ectos followed his father into printing and trained as a litho-printer. Father and

Billets were fairly primitive at first. Ectos Maffuniades (front middle) pictured with his comrades in their tent at Colchester, 1914.

The men of Ectos Maffuniades' company outside their mess tent at Colchester.

son had a print works in Paxton Road on the eve of the Great War, a location now close to the modern White Hart Lane. The Whitbread Brewery was only a few hundred yards away, and it is quite possible it was a major customer of the family concern.

When the war broke out in August 1914 local communities in London were keen to support the war effort. Throughout London there were localised Territorial battalions of the London Regiment, but the only 'regular' infantry regiment connected with the city was the Royal Fusiliers. Local London battalions soon filled up with recruits, and the Royal Fusiliers, a large regiment with four regular battalions and three reserve, also began to expand as early as August 1914, prior to Lord Kitchener, Secretary of State for War, calling for 100,000 Volunteers in September 1914. Ectos Maffuniades joined the 10th Battalion Royal Fusiliers in late August 1914, being its 466th recruit. The 10th was an unusual battalion which had been formed on the wishes of Sir Henry Rawlinson, then Director of Recruiting and later commander of the Fourth Army on the Somme. In a letter less than ten days after the outbreak of the war, Rawlinson suggested to Major the Honourable R. White that, 'many City employees who would

Soldiering wasn't just marching and bayonet drill – men of the 'Stockbrokers' on fatigues.

be willing to enlist if they were assured that they would serve with their friends'.[1] White began collecting names and opened the battalion for recruitment officially on 21 August, when more than 200 enlisted. By 27 August it was more than 1,700 strong and was called the 'Stockbrokers' Battalion', although only a minority of the originals were men who worked in the City's financial institutions.

> The numbers speak for themselves; but they represent the result of a careful selection among the eager flock who presented themselves. Parading in all sorts of clothing, from silk hats and morning coats to caps and Norfolk jackets, the battalion was inspected . . . by Lord Roberts in Temple Gardens, and marched thence to the Tower Ditch, where they were sworn in by the Lord Mayor.[2]

Ectos left for Colchester with his battalion, where they went into training and joined the 18th (Eastern) Division, an infantry division comprising battalions raised in the Home Counties, then assembling in the barracks there. Within a few weeks of their formation the 'New Army' was formed by Lord Kitchener, promoted by that famous poster of him calling the young men of Britain to enlist. A great success, with the influx of so many volunteers as a result of this campaign, and the creation of new battalions in regiments right across Britain, there was a great shortage of uniforms, equipment and weapons. Contemporary photographs of the 10th Battalion show this was not so much of a problem, possibly because of their formation prior to the main call for recruits. Training continued into 1915, when they now moved to Salisbury Plain and joined the 37th Division, which had the nickname the 'English Division' as it comprised units from every part of England. By the summer of 1915 the battalion was ready for overseas service, and Ectos and his comrades found themselves departing for Boulogne via Folkestone on 30 July 1915.

Their war began, like many other battalions at this time, in a rest camp outside the town, a short march from the docks. The next day they entrained and moved nearer to the front, getting out of the train at Watten, north of St Omer, and marching to Hazebroucke. Here they got their first experience of the cobbled roads, something mentioned in the battalion War Diary. Cobbles are tricky to walk on in the best of situations, but to march for an hour at a time, with a 10-minute rest, and in British Army boots with their metal studs on the soles was taxing for even the fittest of men the first time it was experienced. In the small village of St Sylvestre they paraded and were inspected by General Plumer, then commanding the Second

Lunch break on a route march of the 'Stockbrokers'. The middle-class background of the battalion is evident in that several men are already officer cadets, as shown by the white band on their caps.

Trench digging, 1915. A few short weeks later the men would be doing this for real in the front line of Northern France.

Filling bags with straw in preparation for bayonet drill. The reality was that most men would never use their bayonet in combat.

Army in Northern France, which their division had now joined. The next few days saw men from the battalion, Ectos among them, being sent to the front line around the French town of Armentières for instruction into the day-to-day activities of trench warfare. The town had become famous because of the well-known soldier's song 'Mademoiselle from Armentières', but it had not seen any major fighting since October 1914. The front lines had been established east of the town around the village of Houplines and some outlying suburbs, and in fact they would not move or change until the final year of the war. It was a very 'quiet' sector, but one that the Army used as a so-called 'Nursery Sector' where units fresh from Britain, like Ectos and the 'Stockbrokers', could be given hands-on training. They would learn how to relieve a battalion in the front line, about trench equipment and stores and get acclimatised to the day-to-day activities without being in an area of major operations, and thus the risk of casualties was hopefully fairly small.

After this rapid induction the battalion came out of the trenches and was back on the railways of France heading for Doullens. From here they marched towards the front line north of the Somme, close to the village of Foncquevillers (or 'Funky-villas' to the troops, who always had problems

A communication trench in Foncquevillers ('Funky-villas' to the troops) used by Ectos and his comrades of the 'Stockbrokers' when they took over this sector from the French in 1915.

pronouncing French place names and often corrupted them). This sector was in the process of being taken over from the French army as the British extended their line south. On 3 September 1915 the 10th Royal Fusiliers relieved the 355th Regiment d'Infanterie in the front line at Foncquevillers. The 355th was a regiment raised in the Marne department of France that had fought in the 1914 campaign, and had occupied the trenches here and around neighbouring Monchy au Bois since early 1915.[3] They had pretty much operated a 'live and let live' philosophy here, and had done little to add to or improve the infrastructure of the front-line positions. The Adjutant recorded: 'weather very wet. Trenches in good order . . . dugouts in village had been almost entirely destroyed by shell fire. No civilians here.'[4]

This next period of the battalion's experiences would be, unbeknown to Ectos and his comrades, an insight into what was to come in terms of the type of trench warfare they were now engaged in. Since landing in France the battalion had lost three men killed and ten wounded. This for only a handful of days in the trenches, and not one of them killed or wounded in any sort of major battle. But activity was about to increase. On 29 September their experience took a new turn with a raid into no-man's-land. Raiding was increasingly becoming part of the daily activity of warfare on the Western Front, as both sides attempted to influence, more than win the deadlock by carrying out these small-scale operations. The 10th Royal Fusiliers carried out a typical example: 'A patrol of 1 officer, 9 snipers and 4 bombers during night attack enemy listening post and accounted for one German. Fire was opened on them from enemy trenches – 2/Lt Haviland wounded. 1 NCO missing.'[5]

The point of these raids were to keep the enemy on their toes, gather intelligence about the location of enemy positions and ensure that there were men trained in the battalion able to operate at night, and in particular be familiar with no-man's-land on the battalion's front in darkness. The British felt this always gave them the upper hand, and raids could be small affairs like this one, or much larger when an entry was made into the enemy's positions with the intention of destroying a specific target, or gathering intelligence information from documents that might be found and, even better, grabbing a prisoner who could be brought back for interrogation. It is clear that the 10th Royal Fusiliers were getting adept at these tactics as their War Diary shows increased activity of this type for the rest of 1915. In October they did a wide sweep of no-man's-land at night on several occasions, gathering vital information for headquarters. The battalion snipers were also active, and on one occasion in November a party of three of them crept into an excellent firing position close to the German lines opposite Foncquevillers and shot three German soldiers. British snipers were trained to target officers or senior Non Commissioned Officers, so the loss of three such men in one day must have been of some effect. After one encounter the body of a dead German soldier was found, identifying him as a soldier of the 3rd Battalion 169th Reserve Infantry Regiment, a unit recruited in Baden. In December the same snipers, to show what a dominance they had of this sector, crawled out across no-man's-land and placed a wooden board on the German barbed wire with text picked up from a newspaper that implied Germany was ready to talk peace. The board soon disappeared, but it showed how proficient these men had become in fieldcraft on the battlefield.

No daily records survive for all these activities within the battalion, save a mention of them in the battalion War Diary, so it is not known who actually took part in these raids. The success of them in the 10th Royal

The German trench system in front of Gommecourt, which Ectos and the men of the 'Stockbrokers' Battalion' raided in January 1916.

Fusilier would seem to indicate that a regular group of men took part, but in reality it was more likely that a greater spread of men would be used eventually with the idea of training up as many potential raiders as possible. Records of the battalion certainly indicate Ectos Maffuniades took part, but the first mention of him in a raid was in January 1916. At this time the battalion was once again holding the trenches at Foncquevillers, directly opposite a stretch of woodland marked on British maps as Gommecourt Wood, close to the village of Gommecourt. The positions here were separated by a low valley, which was often damp, wet and muddy, but: 'a patrol sent out last night heard sounds of the enemy walking through water. German sentries in their listening posts were also heard talking. Reports received . . . lead to the belief that the Germans are not holding their front trenches very strongly'.[6] Getting closer for a better look was difficult in these weather conditions, so instead a full-scale raid was decided upon to enter the German trenches and verify this for certain. The raid was to be commanded by one of the company commanders, Captain Frederick

Russell Roberts, and Ectos was a member of the raiding party. The War Diary recorded on 13 January 1916:

a strong patrol was sent out from Trench 51 early this morning . . . with the intention of entering the enemy's trenches . . . They proceeded to the Sunken Road and then headed straight for the enemy's wire to a point where a gap in the wire was known to exist as a result of reconnaissance on preceding nights. On arrival at the wire however the gap was found to have been closed. The men told off previously as wire cutters thereupon started work on the wire in the place where the gap had been. They had only been at the work a short time when what sounded like a voice or voices was heard close by to say something in German. It was not a challenge but immediately rifle fire was opened up on the wire cutters from a very close range. Captain Roberts was severely wounded by the first shot and 3 of the men were wounded by a bomb. Realising that a surprise attack was out of the question and also on account of the great thickness and depth of the wire the party was ordered to retire. The party returned to our lines shortly afterwards. The scheme had been carefully thought out in every detail before it was undertaken and a moonless stormy night selected for the enterprise, and the faces of the men had even been blackened to minimise the risk of detection. Although it ended in failure much useful knowledge and experience was gained at a small loss.[7]

Roberts was so badly hit that he could not move back by himself. Ectos immediately stepped in. Roberts later wrote:

I shall never forget your son's bravery and forgetfulness of self on that unfortunate night when we failed to get into the Boche trenches, and his efforts to carry me in. The Germans were not 30 yards away, but he took no more notice of the danger than if he had been at home, he was so absolutely fearless.[8]

One of his comrades later wrote to his parents in Tottenham:

The bombing party, under Captain Roberts, set out under cover of darkness, and soon reached the wire entanglements. Wire-cutters were soon set to work, but were heard by the German sentries in a listening post nearby; after challenging, the German sentries fired and threw bombs. One of the bombs fell close to Captain Roberts, and although wounded in two places by rifle fire, he immediately picked it up to throw it back to the German post. Unhappily it exploded in his hand, and he sustained severe wounds and a shattered hand. Although suffering great agony, the Captain uttered no sound which would reveal the position of the bombing party, and quietly gave the order to retire. The party were crawling off when Private Maffuniades was struck on the head by a bomb, which fortunately did not explode, and only stunned him for a few minutes. On coming to, he resumed his crawl, and discovered Captain Roberts lying so badly wounded that he was unable to move. The others of the party were some distance off by this time, and it was impossible for Private Maffuniades to attract their attention without shouting, so under a hail of rifle-fire bombs, he half-carried and half-dragged the Captain back towards the British lines; a minute or two later, when firing died down, a German patrol came out, hoping to secure prisoners, but Maffuniades, with the Captain on his back, managed to evade them, and eventually reached the British lines in an exhausted condition.[9]

For his bravery that day, Ectos was awarded a Distinguished Conduct Medal in March 1916, and the man he saved was awarded the Military Cross. Roberts would never serve again because of his injuries, but he did survive the war – his life saved by Ectos' quick thinking and bravery. The citation for his DCM reads: 'For conspicuous gallantry in carrying a wounded comrade, at great personal risk, into a place of safety. On a previous occasion he remained out alone with his Captain, who was wounded, dragged him a distance of 100 yards into a place of comparative safety, and remained with him till stretcher-bearers arrived.'[10] The DCM was a medal only awarded to ordinary soldiers, not officers, and it was second only to the Victoria Cross, so was not issued lightly. It had been introduced during the Crimean War, and originally came with a life pension but the huge number issued in the Great War meant that the War Office quickly abandoned that policy.

The great siege of the Western Front continued. In February Ectos moved with his battalion to a new sector further north, nearer to Arras. By this stage Arras had been taken over by British troops and the trenches that extended from the city down to the Somme were now part of the extended British line. On 11 February the 10th Royal Fusiliers therefore took over trenches close to the village of Bellacourt.

The country hereabouts is a succession of ridges with a chalksoil. About 500 yards separate the opposing front line trenches and the Germans are at a somewhat lower altitude than ours . . . Rations are taken to Bellacourt on limber wagons daily and all food cooked there and taken up to the trenches by carrying parties from the support company. Water is carried up at the same time. The 2nd Class road leading to the trenches, owing to not having been made for the heavy military traffic which passes over it, is in a bad condition and no amount of patching will cause any great improvement. The water supply is poor and is obtained from spring fed wells. Owing to the chalky nature of the soil, the water is very clear and has a large calcium deposit.[11]

The battalion imposed the regime they had developed at Foncquevillers and patrol work began in earnest. It proved a quieter sector than the previous one, but as each week went by a handful of men were killed, and three or four times that number wounded. By March 1916 the battalion was greatly depleted; it had arrived at full strength of over 1,100 officers and men in July 1915, and now it was reduced to around 800 all ranks. Ectos and his comrades were taken out of the trenches and sent to a rest area near Abbeville. Following some time let loose on the town, a concerted programme of training followed in a small village in the Picardy countryside. While it was hard work, it was a welcome break from the monotony of trench warfare. Replacement drafts brought the battalion back up to strength, and indeed the Adjutant remarked at this time just how healthy the battalion was. Battle casualties aside:

only 89 cases of sickness have been evacuated since arrival of the battalion overseas on July 30th 1915. This is largely due to two causes . . . During the period of training in England all men who were immature or showed signs of weakness were promptly weeded out and posted to the Reserve Unit . . . [also] by detention and treatment in the Regimental Aid Post such men as require only a short of period of rest. This obviates the necessity of evacuating them and consequent loss to the battalion for a lengthy period.[12]

This long period of rest and training came to an end in late April 1916, when the battalion returned to the battlefield. They took over another new sector, this time close to the village of Berles au Bois, and opposite Monchy au Bois. The trenches here were the closest together they had ever experienced, with British and German positions separated only by 32yd of

French soil. It would soon see the worst day, casualty wise, the battalion had suffered since arrival in France. On 4 May 1916 the Germans laid down a heavy bombardment of the positions held by the 10th Royal Fusiliers; a form of 'box barrage' fell on their trenches, cutting off the telephone communications. It appeared that the Germans were about to raid, but no raid came despite the sight of ladders in the German trenches. Casualties amounted to six dead and fifty-one wounded. While for the next few weeks casualties never reached that total again, it was clear that the German artillery were much more active here and the War Diary notes far more casualties from shell fire. On 28 May it recorded: 'about 17 shells thought to have been fired from a 150mm gun fell on the left centre company Supports and Trench 99 early this morning'.[13] One man was recorded as a casualty: Private Ectos Maffuniades. Wounded, he died of his injuries at the aid post in Berles au Bois a short time afterwards and was buried in the churchyard in the village. One of his comrades wrote home: 'his absolute disregard of danger, the wonderful coolness under fire, his willingness to undertake any kind of work, made him popular as a man, and as a hero his name will be treasured by the battalion and by those who knew him'.[14]

After ten months in the firing line, living through a typical period of static trench warfare, Ectos had become a victim of the daily attrition of the Western Front. By the close of the war the 10th Royal Fusiliers had suffered

A typical view across no-man's-land, south of Arras, 1916.

The memorial plaque, often called a 'dead man's penny', given to the parents of Ectos Maffuniades in the 1920s. It is now in the collection of the Royal Fusiliers at the Tower of London.

a total of 2,647 casualties.[15] They had taken part in major fighting on the Somme in 1916, at Arras and Ypres in 1917 and in the final battles on the Western Front. However, the majority of this total was not made up of men who had died going headlong into a charge, but who fell in a quiet corner of the Western Front. In that respect Ectos Maffuniades was arguably more typical of the generation that died in the Great War.

Researching Ectos Maffuniades

Like many thousands of soldiers who served in the Great War, the official paper trail for Ectos Maffuniades is limited as his records were

Alexis Ectos Maffuniades' portrait in the Roll of Honour. (Geoff Bridger)

lost in the bombing that affected personnel records during the Second World War. A search at TNA or on Ancestry results in locating his Medal Index Card, which gives his date of overseas service, and using the references on the card the actual medal rolls in WO329 at TNA can then also be consulted. For men like Ectos, who served in the Royal Fusiliers, not only are the battalions of the regiment they served in records in these rolls but also the exact dates of overseas service. While the Royal Fusiliers record office was not unique in doing this, it was sadly rare and the majority of regimental medal rolls do not contain this amount of detail.

To reconstruct his service the starting place was looking into his background. Searching the Internet soon shows reference to the Greek community in London, and using Google Maps and Google Street View it was possible to trace the places where he had lived, and where the family had established their print shops; in one case the original shop front was intact and while now advertising a very different business, it was possible to imagine Ectos and his father at work there. Doing this also highlighted that their business was close to the Whitbread Brewery, which may have been one of their potential, and perhaps lucrative, business clients.

For his war service the 10th Battalion Royal Fusiliers War Diary proved especially detailed. Some diaries can be very brief, and not much more of a list of places where the unit was located. This diary, possibly because it covers a period when the battalion was still in its 'original' formation, and prior to any involvement in big battles, seems to have been an extension of the Adjutant's personal diary, recording many small details. Such diaries can prove useful for helping to reconstruct what an ancestor did when he was overseas, and the sort of things he saw and experienced. While not every regiment published one, H.C. O'Neill's *The Royal Fusiliers in the Great War* proved a helpful addition to the War Diary, especially on the early history of the battalion prior to going to France, something not covered in the diary. Many of these histories have now been reprinted or are available online as digitised books from sources like Project Gutenberg. Both the Imperial War and National Army Museums have good collections of such histories in their libraries, which can be visited by appointment.

After the Great War many rolls of honour were published. The majority were aimed at the families of officers, as we have seen from other chapters in this book, who had the money to purchase entries in them. One open to anyone, irrespective of background, was De Ruvigny's *The Roll of Honour*. Little is known about either the author or publisher of this work, but it ran into several volumes and work on it began before the end of the war. Copies are often available in reference libraries, and the complete set has been reprinted, but it has also been digitised and is online at Ancestry. A search under surname here indicated an entry for Ectos Maffuniades, which filled in many gaps about his background and also provided some first-hand accounts of his act of bravery and the circumstances of his death. His entry also contained a portrait photograph.

Details of gallantry medals, such as the Distinguished Conduct Medal awarded to Ectos Maffuniades, are contained in Index Cards held on microfiche at TNA and also online at Ancestry. These provide the basic military details about the man, and what date the award was announced in the *London Gazette*. This can be looked up online at the *London Gazette* website, where the full edition can be downloaded. Not all gallantry medals had published citations, and sadly all the recommendations for Great War honours and awards were lost in bombing during the Second World War.

Notes

1. H.C. O'Neill, *The Royal Fusiliers in the Great War* (Heinemann, 1922), p. 10.
2. Ibid.
3. Anon., *Historique du 355 Regiment d'Infanterie Pendant la Grande Guerre 1914–1918* (Paris, 1920).
4. 10th Battalion Royal Fusiliers War Diary TNA WO95/2532. Crown Copyright.
5. Ibid. The NCO, Lance Corporal W.F. Reay, a married Authorised Clerk in the Stock Exchange from West Brompton, was never found and his name is on the Thiepval Memorial.
6. Ibid.
7. Ibid.
8. De Ruvigny, *The Roll of Honour*, Volume 4 (n.d., n.p.), p. 126.
9. Ibid.
10. *London Gazette*, 15 March 1916, p. 2891.
11. 10th Battalion Royal Fusiliers War Diary TNA WO95/2532. Crown Copyright.
12. Ibid.
13. Ibid.
14. De Ruvigny, *The Roll of Honour*, p. 126.
15. O'Neill, *The Royal Fusiliers in the Great War*, p. 10.

Chapter Five

BENEATH THE WESTERN FRONT – A TUNNELLER IN FRANCE

William Hackett VC, Royal Engineers

The Great War has often been likened to a huge siege. Opposing sides entrenched along hundreds of miles of Northern France and Belgium saw Germany and the Allies deadlocked for much of the conflict. With both sides sheltering in trenches, dugouts and strong points, and these positions often being very close together, it increasingly became impossible in some locations on the battlefield to come up above ground level to engage the enemy, and, even more importantly, impossible to attack. If only tens of yards separated both sets of trenches, it meant that any attacking force would normally have to advance without artillery support; the distance between friend and foe being so reduced as to make the use of it potentially damaging to those making the attack. In previous sieges, never quite on the scale of this war, it wasn't uncommon for one side to tunnel underneath the other, lay a charge of explosive, destroy a position and allow foot soldiers to advance into the gap. From medieval castle sieges to the blowing of the mine at Petersburg in the American Civil War, it was a battlefield tactic well documented, and one well considered even before the war.

Military Engineering (Part IV): Mining and Demolition was originally published in 1910, and amended in 1915. It detailed the methods to be used in mine warfare, the tactics to be implemented and an outline of the type of warfare it was:

Whether the occasion for the use of military mining arises suddenly . . . or whether it occurs in a regular siege . . . the general principles governing the action of both sides will be the same as they have been hitherto . . . At all times subterranean warfare is a tedious operation to the attacker, but he has much in his favour, so that he should, sooner or later, gain ground . . . In no species of warfare is a clear cool head, combined with decisive and energetic action, more required than in the conduct of operations of this nature.[1]

It even described the types of equipment to be used and grades of explosive to be implemented, right down to the electrical methods that were required. Of course, all this mirrored advancements in civilian mining work, which in the Victorian and Edwardian period had been active: from blowing railway tunnels through mountains in Canada, to working in diamond and tin mines, to construction work on the Manchester sewers and building extensions to the London Underground.

One man who was sure the key to breaking the deadlock on the Western Front was the use of military mining on a grand scale was John Norton Griffiths. Norton Griffiths was a civilian mining engineer who had worked in South Africa, fought in the Boer War and become a Member of Parliament for Wednesbury. On the outbreak of war he had formed the 2nd King Edwards Horse, a cavalry regiment, but had taken to touring the front in his own Rolls-Royce car. Here he saw the realities of what the front had become by early 1915 and came into contact with officers who convinced him that mining, tunnelling, was the way forward. He went to see Lord Kitchener, Secretary of State for War and the War Office to suggest that: 'coal miners and other underground workers should be specially enlisted for this purpose, great stress being laid on the secrecy and silence with which professional "clay kickers" could work'.[2] The term 'clay kickers' referred to a tunnelling method developed in the pre-war period when working in the blue clay beneath London and Manchester. The miner would wear a special pair of boots and be equipped with a special shovel, and be able to cut through the clay at a rapid, and less noisy, rate.

Norton Griffiths had called for the implementation of thousands of tunnellers, but while this was not to be, the War Office approved the formation of the first Tunnelling Companies of the Royal Engineers in February 1915; the first personnel that joined the newly formed 170th Tunnelling Company had five days before been employed on sewer work beneath Liverpool. This was the great attraction of the formation of these units to the War Office: they did not require any additional training as they would basically be carrying out the same sort of work they had done in civilian life. Miners of all sorts would be required, but as mining was a protected occupation which precluded a man from enlisting, the incentive to join would have to be pay. The War Office therefore decided to pay Tunnellers a minimum of 6s a day; compared to just 1s for a basic private in an infantry battalion. In many cases these were wages well above what the miners were being paid by civilian companies, so there was no shortage of enlistees in 1915. But the rapidity with which they arrived on the Western Front did cause problems. For some time Tunnellers still saw themselves as miners, not soldiers. They did not understand they had to salute officers or abide by military law. It was therefore apparent that some degree of military training would be required for the units then forming so that the men knew what their responsibilities as front-line combatants would be. One officer's account from mid-1915 gives an indication of the problems facing these new units on a simple route march at the base:

> When reaching the top of a hill in Rouen, I looked round to see that the party was alright, and to my surprise saw several of the men getting off a bus at the top of the hill and rejoining the file. They had seen the bus at the bottom of the hill and decided it was the easier way, and, as the War Office instructions were just to get the men out, I did not consider this called for any disciplinary action.[3]

One man who joined the Tunnellers at this time was William Hackett. Hackett was a 42-year-old Yorkshire miner who lived and worked in Mexborough, Yorkshire, although originally he was born at Sneinton, near Nottingham. Mexborough in 1915 was a mining community with back-to-back housing and was typical of the sort of place men from tunnelling companies were recruited. Hackett was married to Alice, and had two children born in 1901 and 1903, and he had spent most of his life working in the pits, after an early start in a Nottingham factory. He had never been properly educated and was illiterate, the attestation papers he filed at Doncaster in November 1915 being filled in on his behalf, and the recruiting officer signing the declaration required to join for him. He had previously tried to enlist in the infantry on several occasions but been rejected due to his age and also on medical grounds. But his mining experience made him exactly the sort of man the War Office was looking for to work in the Tunnelling Companies, and three weeks after he joined, and after some

William Hackett VC just prior to going to France, 1915.

basic military training at Chatham, he was in uniform and heading to France.

Here William Hackett joined 181st Tunnelling Company Royal Engineers. A tunnelling company was a small unit, and upon joining he was one of 9 officers and, at full establishment, 283 men. The 181st Tunnelling Company was based at this time at Sailly sur la Lys, a village behind the lines in Northern France. This part of France was very flat, but beneath the sub soil the clay here was suitable for tunnelling, in the same way it was in Flanders just across the border. The front lines here had hardly moved since they became fixed in October 1914, and the Company had established mining galleries in the Red Farm Corner–Well Farm–La Cordonnerie Farm area. Across no-man's-land was the village of Fromelles, and beyond that Aubers Ridge. The ground here had seen heavy fighting in the Battle of Aubers Ridge in May 1915, before Hackett had arrived. Mines had been used in that attack and their craters were still visible. It was known that German pioneers were opposite, also working on galleries, but unlike British miners these men were not necessarily recruited in the same way; the Germans did not specifically choose men with mining backgrounds, just normal engineers and pioneers. This, many British Tunnellers felt, always gave them the upper hand as tunnelling was 'in their blood'. It was this type

Tunnellers at work beneath the Western Front.

of warfare that became Hackett's day-to-day life here for the next six months.

The work of the Tunnelling Companies varied greatly depending on what part of the front they were serving in. In a sector like that around Fromelles the mining was generally targeted at the workings of the Germans, trying to blow in their tunnels and systems before the Germans had the chance to do it themselves. But working in the tunnels themselves was dangerous work on its own. In the clay found here, all the tunnels had to be propped up with timber to stop them collapsing. But collapse they did, causing danger and injury. In addition, poison could build up in the tunnels. This was not gas deliberately sent over by the Germans, but natural gas, in this case carbon monoxide, which built up when the tunnels were formed. Carbon monoxide is a silent killer; it has no smell and cannot easily be detected, and was the cause of many casualties in the early years of tunnelling. It was found that certain small animals could be used to assist in its detection; yellow canaries and mice were the most common. The fumes would affect them much more quickly and if they were seen to collapse in their cages, the men working in that area knew that gas was building up. Canaries had long claws, and it was necessary to keep them regularly clipped otherwise they would grip the perch in their cage in rigor mortis, giving the appearance of still being alive. It was therefore said that the life of a Tunneller depended on the length of a canary's claws. But men being men, they often established a close bond with the animals, and in some cases became reluctant to put them in harm's way.

> One case is on record where . . . a rescue station had only one canary left. This bird had been for a number of months in the . . . dug-out with the mine rescue men, and had been made a pet of. When a blow occurred and they were ordered to take the canary down and test for gas they did so, but hung the cage near an opening of the armoured hose supplying air to the working face, so that whatever happened the canary would get good air![4]

Thankfully, during this time Hackett was with 181st Company around Fromelles and there was only one fatal casualty.[5] While it was hard physical labour, in terms of danger it was a gradual introduction to the life of a Western Front Tunneller.

However, January 1916 brought sad news for William. His son Arthur had followed him into the mines at Mexborough, although only aged 14,

Entrance to a tunnel system on the Western Front.

and had been in an accident with some coal trucks which resulted in him losing his left leg below the knee. William could not get leave to come home and see his son, and being illiterate he asked a fellow Tunneller to write home for him: 'It is very hard to have his leg off but God knows best . . . its very hard for me to be in this foreign land and have a lad placed in hospital . . . I cannot help him but I know you will do all you can'.[6] In later letters from March and April 1916 he said:

> We shall have to look on the bright side of things and pray for the best you know because all our lives are full of troubles and I wish to God they was all over with and the war is only just starting since I have been out here but the young fellow that writes for me says it is only just the same as it was last year but dear Wife there is going to be some bloodshed before so very long they don't intend it going on so very much longer and they all seem to think so too and I don't care how soon because we are all fed up. . . . I hope and trust to God that I will be able to come home safe and sound to be along with you all one day. I hope they will soon shift us from here, for it is not fit for us to be in as we get to dodge the bullets on every side of us coming in at night. I hope you have enjoyed yourself this Easter for we are not

able to go out here but if I lives to pull through I will have a holiday to make up for all this.[7]

The man who wrote the letters wanted to explain how he felt, and said to William's wife: 'I hope Mrs Hackett that the letters I write for your husband is alright, because he never tells me anything to put in. I know it is not like writing one himself and I know it must be very hard lines that he can't write.'[8]

What it must have been like for William to be separated from his family at this time can only be imagined, but there is no indication it affected his work and dedication as a soldier. In April 1916 his unit moved to a new sector around Arras, recently taken over from the French army. The 181st Company were now working on mining galleries in very different ground – chalk. Unlike at Fromelles, this was hard digging, where clay kickers could not operate. It was probably much more like the sort of mining work William had done in Yorkshire.

For a reason not recorded in his service record, William Hackett transferred to the 254th Tunnelling Company Royal Engineers on 15 May 1916. He moved north from Arras to the area around the La Bassée Canal close to the village of Givenchy les la Bassée. Here the 254th Company had been active for some time, working on the mining galleries east of the

The village of Givenchy where Hackett joined the 254th Tunnelling Company in May 1916.

village. Mines had been blown here on several occasions over the past year, and their craters littered the battlefield. The sector had just been occupied by the 11th, 12th and 13th Battalions Royal Sussex Regiment (South Downs), which had been in positions overlooking an older mine crater called The Duck's Bill. Front lines were between 50yd and 100yd apart here, but it was a key position as the village of Givenchy lay on a slight rise, which provided good views towards the town of La Bassée in German hands. On a localised basis both sides had been disputing it since October 1914 and June 1916 was about to see another stage in this battle for the possession and re-possession of high ground. By this stage the 2nd Battalion Royal Welsh Fusiliers were in the line, and on the morning of 22 June 1916 the Germans made the next move. Frank Richards of the battalion later recalled it in his memoirs:

> I arrived back in my dugout and about 1.30am was woken up by a terrific explosion on our right front. The ground shook and rocked as if an earthquake had taken place . . . The company stood-to: we knew that the enemy had exploded a mine on our extreme right but were not sure whether it was in our battalion's area or not.[9]

A bitter fight for the crater followed, for which Richards was later awarded a Distinguished Conduct Medal for his bravery. The battalion lost three officers and fifty-two men killed, plus many more wounded, and the landscape was changed by the creation of what became known as The Red Dragon Crater. But another battle, of a different sort, was taking place beneath the battlefield.

The men of the 254th Tunnelling Company had been working on their mining galleries at the time the mine exploded in the early hours of the morning. The so-called Shaftesbury Shaft the men were working in was 35ft below the surface and timber shored. At the face were five men, William Hackett among them. The explosion of the mine brought down 25ft of the tunnel, trapping the men, although they were physically unharmed. A mine rescue party was immediately put to work, and after two days they broke through a small pocket in the collapsed soil and timber to where the men were located. Hackett made sure three of the men were through, and went back for Private Thomas Collins of the 14th Battalion Welsh Regiment (Swansea Pals) who was seriously injured. William refused to leave Collins, and is said to have shouted 'I am a tunneller, I must look after the others first.' Collins could not be got through the gap, and the working party now had not only the collapse to deal with but also the fact that their mine shaft

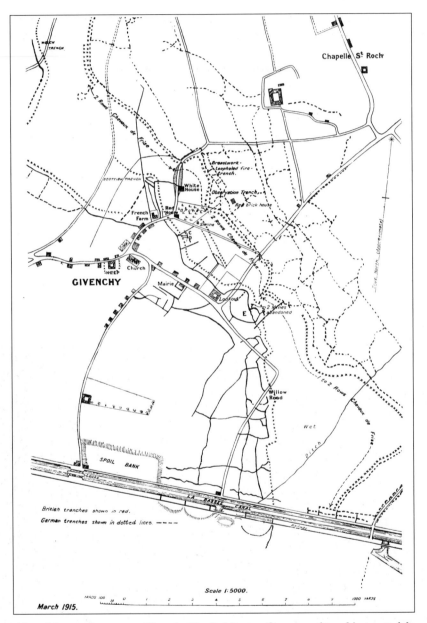

Map of the trench system at Givenchy. The Red Dragon Crater was formed just east of the position marked 'E'.

was coming under fire from artillery and trench mortars. There appears to have been a secondary collapse, and by the time the rescue party got close to Hackett and the injured Collins again, the remainder of the mining gallery had come down and both men were dead. Captain G.M. Edwardes wrote to Alice Hackett a few days later:

> I find it very difficult to express to you adequately the admiration I and all the officers had for the heroic manner in which your husband met his death. Sad as his loss may be to his own people, yet his fearless conduct and wonderful selfsacrifice must always be a source of pride and comfort to you all. Your husband deliberately sacrificed his own life to save his comrades, and even when three or four were saved he refused to save himself because the remaining man was too injured to help himself. He has been recommended for the V.C., that simple medal which represents all that is brave and noble. In token of our esteem, the officers and men are sending you a small gift in the near future, which we trust will be acceptable.[10]

A contemporary illustration from Deeds That Thrill The Empire *showing Hackett carrying out his selfless act of courage.*

Mine rescue on the Western Front, typical of the equipment used following the collapse of Hackett's tunnel.

Up to this point no Tunneller had been awarded a Victoria Cross. In many respects the Tunnellers generally had been short-changed when it came to honours and awards. Their work was considered so secret and as medals were listed in the *London Gazette* often with a citation, it was felt that publishing such details would give too much information to the enemy about what the companies were up to. Because of the circumstances of William Hackett's death, and that all witnesses clearly stated he was unhurt and had deliberately chosen to stay with Collins, the recommendation was widely accepted and William Hackett became the only Tunneller to get the Victoria Cross, albeit posthumously. The official citation read:

> For most conspicuous bravery when entombed with four others in a gallery owing to the explosion of an enemy mine. After working for 20 hours a hole was made through fallen earth and broken timber, and the outside party was met. Sapper Hackett helped three of the men through the hole and could easily have followed, but refused to leave the fourth, who had been seriously injured, saying 'I am a tunneller, I must look after the others first.' Meantime the hole was getting smaller, yet he still refused to leave his injured comrade. Finally the gallery collapsed, and though the rescue party worked desperately for four days the attempt to reach the two men failed. Sapper Hackett, well knowing the nature of sliding earth, the chances against him, deliberately gave his life for his comrade.[11]

Sapper Evans, who had helped his mate William write home to his wife because he was unable to, now found himself penning a very different sort of letter:

> I am most sorry to have to write to you under such circumstances that is to inform you that your Husband Sapper Hackett was Killed in Action on 22nd June but I can tell you that he died a heroes death as brave as any man as died in this war which I hope before long you will hear more about it. And I can tell you your Husbands death is sadly felt as he was respected by all the officers and men of the 254 Company and as for myself I miss him so much as if he was my own Father as you know I used to write his letters for him. And all the boys of his section wish me to send you their best wishes and hope that you and the children will have the best of health and good luck and hope you will try and bear the sad news and they asked me to tell you that you can be proud of the way your husband died as he

View close to the edge of the Red Dragon Crater, 1920s. The memorial to the 55th Division is seen in the background. No trace of the crater remains today.

was a hero if ever there was one. I only wish I could tell it the way it happened but as you know we are not allowed to but if I am spared to come over this lot I will come and see you and let you know all about it. Well Mrs Hackett I must draw to a close by wishing you and the children the best of health and good luck.[12]

The Royal Engineers began a fund to support Alice Hackett and her children; money especially needed as now not only was her husband dead but her son having been injured in the colliery accident was no longer fit to work. In December 1916 she was interviewed by the local press.

Mrs Hackett was asked by the *Times* representative what were her feelings upon learning that her husband had risen to such a height of heroism. 'Well', she said, 'I knew he was no coward. I could never understand the doctors rejecting him on account of his heart. There wasn't much wrong with that, was there? He was always after joining the Army, and I know he tried hard to get into the York and Lancaster Regiment. Only a few weeks before he enlisted, he got cut across the back by a fall of roof in the Manvers Main mine, and had a very narrow escape from death, so the deputy afterwards told me. The deputy wanted him to be taken home at once, but he refused saying he would work the shift out because his missus would be upset if she thought he had been hurt so badly that he had to give up work before the shift was up. That's the sort of man he was. I can just imagine what he would think when he was down in the mine where he met his death. He would think when he heard that another poor fellow was fastened up in there: What would my feelings be if I was lying helpless and nobody would stay with me. I must go to him, even if we both go under.'[13]

The bodies of Thomas Collins and William Hackett were never recovered from the Shaftesbury Shaft beneath the battlefield at Givenchy. After the

William Hackett's wife and children at Mexborough, 1916. (Royal Engineers Museum)

war, with no grave, their names would be added to the requisite memorial to the missing. The criteria for being placed on a memorial in this area is somewhat complex as certain memorials cover specific time frames or cover specific geographic areas, often bordered by rivers or streams. As such both men's names should have been engraved on the Loos Memorial which: 'commemorates over 20,000 officers and men who have no known grave, who fell in the area from the River Lys to the old southern boundary of the First Army, east and west of Grenay'.[14] However, Thomas Collins is commemorated on the Thiepval Memorial in the heart of the Somme battlefields and William Hackett VC on the Ploegsteert Memorial in Belgium. Collins to some degree is an understandable mistake as he was only attached to 254th Tunnelling Company and when he died his battalion was heading south to take part in the Battle of Somme. If his attachment was not known to the War Graves Commission then he would naturally have been commemorated as he was on Thiepval. Why Hackett is on the Ploegsteert Memorial is more of a mystery as this memorial does not commemorate men killed so far into France. It may well just be a clerical error, and in some respects is only a minor point but it would have been significant, perhaps, for Collins and Hackett to be commemorated together as they died and are buried together.

For many years the actions of William Hackett that day were not widely known. His Victoria Cross action did not receive the publicity that many did, again due to the secrecy of the tunnelling units. In the post-war years the events at Givenchy were not mentioned in the official account of military mining, and it took until Alexander Barrie wrote *War Underground* in the 1960s for the work of the Great War Tunnellers to become more widely known. But finally, more than ninety years after he died, a unique memorial will be placed on the Givenchy battlefield in the summer of 2010. A long-term project of military historians Peter Barton and Jeremy Banning, it will focus the visitor's eye on the exact spot in the field where 35ft below Thomas Collins and William Hackett lie buried. Long dead beneath the Western Front, their story lives on and the work of military miners are no longer part of secret history.

Researching William Hackett VC

For many years it was difficult to research the story of Great War Tunnellers in the Royal Engineers as their work remained largely secret up to the release of their War Diaries in the 1960s. Prior to that the main sources were the official account *The Work of the Royal Engineers in the European War 1914–19: Military Mining* and a good unofficial history by two Tunnelling officers, W. Grant Grieve and Bernard Newman, simply entitled *Tunnellers*. The former is difficult to source but can be found in reference libraries such as at the Imperial War Museum; the second volume has been republished. While not every Tunnelling unit, and not every incident involving the Tunnelling companies, is mentioned in these titles they are an excellent starting point. The War Diaries in WO95 at TNA describe the day-to-day activities of the units, but the nature of the work means that some diaries can be quite technical and low on detail in terms of personnel and casualties.

Re-constructing William Hackett's story was greatly helped by the fact that he was awarded a Victoria Cross. Details of such men are normally available widely in publications and on the Internet, but as with many well-known individuals the amount of depth in available accounts is limited. A search of the service records in WO363 at TNA showed that his had survived, but was in a bad state, showing clear signs of having been burnt in the Blitz. However, it provided some vital details of the Tunnelling companies he was posted to, and also information on his age, family and background.

Local newspaper research was especially useful in finding information on Hackett, as his death provoked a widespread reaction in a close-knit mining community. Local newspapers from the period are often found on microfilm in local studies libraries, or in the local county record office. Originals can be seen at the National Newspaper Library at Colindale in London. Print technology had moved on greatly by the time of the Great War, and in some respects local newspapers were more popular than national ones. During the war they printed rolls of honours, obituaries of local casualties and very often carried letters from the front sent in by local men. The plight of Hackett's wife struck a special chord in Mexborough and the local newspapers for some time after his death contained information and photographs about what happened to him.

William Hackett now has his own website,[15] placed online by Peter Barton and Jeremy Banning. Much of the source material used in the telling of Hackett's story is found on this site, along with many of the photographs.

Notes

1. Anon., *Military Engineering (Part IV): Mining and Demolition* (HMSO, 1910, reprinted 1915), pp. 1–2.
2. Anon., *The Work of the Royal Engineers in the European War 1914–19: Military Mining* (W. & J. Mackay & Co., 1922), p. 2.
3. A.D. Lumd, 'The Troubles and Tribulations of a Newly Recruited Tunnelling Officer' (Tunnellers Old Comrades Association Bulletin, n.d.), p. 44.
4. Anon., *The Work of the Royal Engineers*, pp. 69–70.
5. Sapper E. Jones, died 17 April 1916, buried at Aubigny Communal Cemetery Extension. Found using Geoff's Search Engine at: www.hut-six.co.uk/cgi-bin/search1421.php; accessed 1 March 2010.
6. From letters in the collection of the Royal Engineers Museum, Chatham.
7. Ibid.
8. Ibid.
9. Frank Richards, *Old Soldiers Never Die* (annotated version Krijnen & Langley, 2004, originally published 1933), p. 120.
10. From papers in the Hackett family.
11. *London Gazette*, 1916.
12. From papers in the Hackett family.
13. *Mexborough and Swinton Times*, 2 December 1916.
14. Commonwealth War Graves Commission website at: www.cwgc.org; accessed 1 March 2010.
15. www.tunnellersmemorial.com.

Chapter Six

DIED OF WOUNDS AT THE BASE
The Short War of Rifleman Francis Davies

As the Great War moved towards its third year, the War Office looked back at the huge casualty figures of 1914 and 1915, and realised that the flow of volunteers was gradually diminishing. Newspapers were forever full of casualty lists, and it was putting off the young men of Britain from stepping forward and joining up, something they had been all too keen to do before the costly battles that had caused these lists. It was predicted that the trickle of volunteers would end altogether sometime the following year, and that to replace these losses some form of universal conscription would have to be implemented. To try and bring in one last wave of volunteers, Edward Stanley, 17th Lord Derby, became Director General of Recruiting in October 1915. He implemented the Lord Derby Scheme where men of military age from 18 to 40 could register their willingness to enlist, but could defer that enlistment for some months, return to their civilian occupation and wait until the War Office actually needed them. They could chose which regiment to join, and were given a badge and an armband to wear to show they had registered. More than 2 million men registered under the scheme until it was closed in December 1915.

One young man the Lord Derby Scheme appealed to was Francis Hansell Davies. Frank to his family, he had been born in Piccadilly in London in 1893, and grew up in North London. His father was a groom and later foreman of stables, and the family lived in a newly built apartment block alongside Pentonville Prison. In the Edwardian period they moved to

Frank Davies, 1915. At this time he was undertaking vital war work for which he received the badge visible on his lapel to indicate he was doing his 'bit'.

50 Lawford Road, Kentish Town, a house made famous many years later when the author George Orwell lived there in the mid-1930s, and it was here that Frank grew up with his brothers James and Samuel. Sam was six years older than Frank, and James three years younger, and by 1914 all three were working in the city of London, Sam being married and now living in Camden Town. On the outbreak of war, although he was the youngest, James joined the 18th Battalion London Regiment (London Irish Rifles). Frank and Sam were both in good jobs, and Frank was now dating a young local girl, Gertrude. Initially they held back until the Lord Derby Scheme

was introduced and both enlisted under it in late 1915. Frank found himself called into the Army in April 1916 and joined the Rifle Brigade, a regiment based in Winchester but which had traditionally recruited in North London. He was first posted to their depot and then to a training camp at Seaford in Sussex, where he joined the 15th Battalion Rifle Brigade. He later wrote to his parents, describing the date he had attested for duty: 'The bands played us from the Horse Guards to Waterloo last Thursday and another band met us at Winchester and played us to Barracks . . . As soon as we arrived at Winchester (200 of us) we were all served out with our uniforms – and plenty of them too.'[1]

This poor image is the only one known to survive that shows Frank (right) and his 'best girl' Gertrude, in 1915 not long after his brother Jim had joined the London Irish Rifles.

Training was fairly basic; the men were taught to march, fire their weapons and do bayonet drill. Although gas was now a feature of everyday life at the front, gas training was rarely conducted in Britain at this point, and it is likely Frank did not see a gas mask until he got to France. Although Seaford Camp had been in use since the start of the war, accommodation was in tents, not huts. 'Sleeping under canvas is not at all to my liking. There are 10 of us in a tent with our rifles, kit and equipment, with a straw mattress, and consequently we are packed like sardines and haven't an inch to move. Above all it is not a full size tent.'[2] Eventually Frank was moved into a hut, but by the summer of 1916 conscription was beginning, and more and more men were coming into the camp. 'There have been over 1000 new recruits come down . . . and more coming tomorrow – I would rather work on a drilling machine after all. Six silly fools who came down a week or so ago deserted a day after their arrival, but have not yet been caught – they stand no chance of getting away.'[3]

The family house at 50 Lawford Road, Kentish Town. The Blue Plaque records a later resident of the house, author George Orwell. (Photograph: Teri Murphy)

On 1 July 1916 the Battle of the Somme began in Northern France. Operations went badly wrong for the British Army, with more than 57,000 casualties on this day alone, and battalions of the Rifle Brigade were involved from the start. Depots like those at Seaford supplied the replacements for these casualties and gradually Frank saw men posted out to the Western Front. He was selected in late July, but initially he did not pass the medical and was held back. By now his brother James was in France with the London Irish, and no doubt Frank's parents were worried another son might be going to the front. In mid-August he wrote home:

> you musn't be surprised if you get a card from me at any time to say that we are leaving Seaford to finish our training in France. Quite possibly it will be this week. I do not mind going at all as I very much doubt if we shall see any farther than the Base, but if ever we do I shall mind doing a bit of fighting.[4]

Frank's brother Sam (back row, far right) convalescing from wounds while serving in the East Surrey Regiment.

The move to France came quicker than Frank realised. On Monday 28 August 1916 he found himself with the draft from Seaford at Southampton docks. Under the charge of a handful of officers returning to France and some senior Non Commissioned Officers, they had been given a special rail warrant to travel. He just had time to send a farewell postcard to his parents: 'Just a hurried line to let you know I am now on my way. I did not know for certain till this morning & we left Seaford Station at 12 o'clock after a busy morning. We had a very grand send off (about, I should think 1000 of us). Will write first opportunity. Am feeling A1.'[5]

At Southampton the draft was handed over to a Draft Conducting Officer. These men were permanently based at ports to accompany drafts of replacements across ensuring that they embarked correctly, all present and accounted for and when they got to France were disembarked and sent to a rest camp or put on the first train to an Infantry Base Depot. Very often these officers were medically downgraded men who had served in France earlier in the war, and had been wounded or gassed so seriously they were now not fit to serve on the front line. One can only imagine what they made of eager young recruits like Frank. Once aboard the ship, there was little else for the men to do except stash their rifle and equipment. Normally they would be allowed to go up on deck, and as the ship pulled out onto Southampton water, thoughts of home and 'Merry England' and whether they would ever see it again must have passed through the minds of all those present crossing over for the first time.

On arrival at Le Havre, the draft were escorted off to the ship and then formed up. Instead of moving to one of the main Base Depots at Rouen, they had been detailed to the nearest Infantry Base Depot at Le Havre, which was located on the rising ground beyond the town. From the port they marched to the camp, through the streets of Le Havre and into the countryside. As new men they no doubt believed the French people would still be in the streets upon their arrival, waving them on and calling cheery messages, as they had done to the Old Contemptibles in 1914 and the first influx of volunteers in 1915. But more than two years into the war France was war weary. More than ½ million Frenchmen had died since August 1914, and the current year had nearly seen defeat at Verdun. The population, if they paid any attention at all, just viewed them as yet another group of Tommies heading to the front. If Frank and his comrades had been paying attention they would have noticed that the civilians they did encounter were from several distinct groups; children, young women and old men and women. They saw no one of

One of Frank's letters written from the camp at Le Havre, not long after his arrival in France.

their own age; all the young men being on war service. Many veterans remembered what a strange, and sometimes shocking site this was at times.

At the Infantry Base Depot, a large establishment capable of housing several thousand soldiers in wooden huts, Frank was able to write to his parents the next day and tell them he had arrived safely. His first note was just on a scrap of paper, and it took him a few days to get his bearings at this huge camp. Eventually he found the Young Man's Christian Association (YMCA) Hut, a location that was often frequented by new arrivals like Frank. Here there was a canteen where soldiers could get tea and a handful of snacks, but more importantly free writing paper and envelopes were provided. Frank had maintained close contact with his parents and was determined to do this on active service, so at the first opportunity no doubt got himself a brew and sat down to write home; the huts had tables and chairs where the men could write, and there were civilian workers of the YMCA on hand and religious representatives if the soldier needed any spiritual guidance or help, or just a kind word. On colourful YMCA paper, his first proper letter from Le Havre read: 'Just a line to let you know that I have arrived safely in France at a Rest Camp. Please note that I am now in the 10th Battalion. We had a very good passage, but the weather is terrible . . . The food is very good indeed in fact everything is A1. I am ditto.'[6]

Typically soldiers would spend upwards of a week in an Infantry Base Depot, awaiting posting to a battalion at the front line. Frank had already been officially posted to the 10th Battalion, which was then on the Somme front having just moved down from Ypres. His time at the Base would have involved extra training, particularly on the use of anti-gas equipment which was usually not part of the training syllabus in Britain. Post during the war was always good, and within a couple of days letters were arriving from home which he could reply to.

> Many thanks for your letter received tonight . . . I daresay you were surprised to hear that I had left England, but I don't yet realise I am in France. One thing we do notice is that we are treated much better in every way. We were each given two packets of cigarettes and a box of matches last Wednesday. I think we shall be moved from here within the next day or so. Do not write again until I give you a new address.[7]

Frank was right, he was on the move. With the time at the Base at an end, he was posted to the front. The journey would be by train, and he marched out of the camp at Le Havre to the nearest railway station. Here full-sized steam trains, operated by the Railway Operation Division of the Royal Engineers, were waiting. It was hardly a luxurious ride, as the men like Frank were loaded into wooden box cars on which were stencilled the French legend 'Hommes 40, Cheveux 8': forty men or eight horses. If Frank had thought the tents at Seaford cramped, that was nothing compared to the experience in the troops trains. Packed in, there was little room to do much except stand. One benefit was that very often the trains would travel so slowly that soldiers could leap out when they required a 'call of nature', find a suitable bush and be able to run and catch the train again. Some veterans even claimed there was time to nip to the nearest cafe, have an omelette and then rejoin the ride, although that is likely to be the stuff of myths!

One last-minute change was that Frank was no longer destined for the 10th Battalion; he was instead posted to the 8th Battalion, part of 14th (Light) Division. This formation, made up of light infantry units such as the Rifle Brigade, King's Royal Rifle Corps and several battalions of Light Infantry regiments, had been in France since mid-1915 and had fought extensively at Ypres and had just come down from Arras. The battalion had suffered some losses on the Somme in August 1916, and Frank was destined to join them as a replacement. His draft reached the railhead at Airaines, and then marched down to the small village of Leleu, a few miles to the south, where the 8th Rifle Brigade War Diary[8] recorded that they joined as a group of fifty men on 5 September 1916. The battalion was out on rest in this small Picardy village, quite some distance from the front. There was little sign of the war directly, although the sound of bombardments in the distance could no doubt be heard. Leleu was a village set in a river valley, populated with small farms that contained wattle-and-daub-style barns where the men slept. The War Diary further records that on 6 September Frank and his fellow members of the draft were inspected by the Medical Officer. Now that conscription was in full swing, Medical Officers were seemingly sceptical that 'new' men were up to the same standards as the volunteers they were used to, but Frank passed muster.

On the 8 September Frank was able to send a postcard home to his parents. No letters survive from the period at Leleu, and it is possible he had no time to write them. A new man in an unfamiliar unit, he probably found himself put to duty on all sorts of tasks and although the battalion as a whole was out on 'rest', rest never really was that in the Army; there was

NOTHING is to be written on this side except the date and signature of the sender. Sentences not required may be erased. If anything else is added the post card will be destroyed.

I am quite well.

I have been admitted into hospital

{ *sick* } *and am going on well.*
{ *wounded* } *and hope to be discharged soon.*

I am being sent down to the base.

I have received your { *letter dated* _____
{ *telegram* „ _____
{ *parcel* „ _____

Letter follows at first opportunity.

I have received no letter from you

{ *lately.*
{ *for a long time.*

Signature only. } Frank

Date 1st Sept '16

[Postage must be prepaid on any letter or post card addressed to the sender of this card.]

93509) Wt. W3497 293 1,125m. 6/16 J. J. K. & Co., Ltd.

Written only a couple of days before he went over the top, this brief Field Service Postcard was one of Frank's last letters home.

always something that needed doing. Fatigues, from digging latrines to repairing buildings and unloading stores, were the lot of the infantry soldier, and especially the newer members of a battalion. Instead of a letter, Frank was able to acquire a Field Service Postcard. These pre-printed cards were provided free by the Army so a soldier could let family know he was okay with the minimum of effort. A series of bland statements were printed on the card, and you simply struck out the ones that did not apply. Frank's card read, 'I am quite well . . . Letter follows at first opportunity.' Soldiers were not allowed to write anything else on the card, except being able to sign and date it, and put the address on the other side. Printed at the top in bold was 'If anything else is added the post card will be destroyed.' At least his parents knew he was okay, but many families came to realise that the arrival of a card like this meant that their loved one was too busy to write, and if he was too busy, what was he doing?

While work was indeed filling much of his time, he finally got a chance to write a letter the next day. On thin paper he had managed to scrounge from somewhere, it read:

The basilica or 'Leaning Virgin' of Albert on the Somme, a familiar landmark that Frank saw as he moved up to the front in September 1916.

you are no doubt anxiously awaiting a letter from me. Well I am pleased to say that I am quite alright and after a good deal of travelling have joined the 8th Battalion. We are present resting in billets. I am writing this in the orchard . . . We have come through some lovely country in our travels and you would not believe the tremendous amount of fruit about. As you know we cannot say much in a letter and I am quite at a loss what to write. I am feeling very fit and well.[9]

Within a couple of days the battalion was on the move again. On 10 September a huge convoy of forty-three lorries, driven by men in the Army Service Corps, arrived and the men piled in. With no suspension and solid tires, these lorries were not exactly a blessing, but a new operation was in hand on the Somme and units had to be rushed in to take part, the 8th Rifle Brigade among them. Their journey took them across the valley of the River Somme between Abbeville and Amiens, and then through the many small villages to Dernancourt, close to the town of Albert. Here they went into billets; very different from Leleu, Dernancourt showed considerable signs of shell fire and damage. From the village Frank and his comrades would have been able to see the basilica, the church in Albert, the tower of which was topped with a golden figure of Mary with her arms out holding

The smashed trees of Delville Wood which Frank moved past before going into action at Flers-Courcelette on 15 September 1916.

the infant Jesus. This church, only finished in 1912, had been hit by a shell in January 1915 and thereafter the figure of Mary hung at a roughly 90° angle. It was a familiar landmark to men like Frank who served on the Somme, who called it the 'Golden Virgin' or 'Leaning Virgin'. Dernancourt in September 1916 contained a handful of Australian units, pulling out of the Somme area after nearly two months of combat. One of them might have told Frank of the name they gave the figure of Mary – Fanny Durack.[10] They had named the landmark after a female Australian Olympic swimmer who had won a gold medal for the country in the 1912 Olympics; they thought it looked like Fanny diving into a swimming pool!

From Dernancourt they marched up to a rest camp near the village of Fricourt. This had been in German hands at the beginning of the battle, but had been captured in July. Temporary camps had sprung up around it in hollows, for units going to and from the front line. Officers from the battalion left the unit here to go and reconnoitre the ground around the infamous Delville Wood, known as 'Devil's Wood' to the men because of the horrific nature of the fighting there. The ground was smashed to pieces and Delville was a wood in name only. Very few landmarks indicated any idea of geography, so when the battalion moved up at 5 pm on 12 September they stopped for a tea break and were met by guides who would see them up to the right part of the battlefield; this tactic was increasingly in use as the battlefield became confused and often unrecognisable, especially at night and during major operations like the Somme. Early that evening they reached the trenches north-east of the wood, where the next morning, settled into the front line close to Brown Trench, they could see the ruins of the village of Ginchy, in German hands, to their right and the ruined and smashed roof-tops of Flers ahead of them, some way across the fields.

Frank now found himself thrown in the deep end. Normally a unit would have the chance to acclimatise to the conditions of the battlefield, to get used to life in the trenches, and then take part in a major battle. Training prepared a soldier to a certain degree, but only experience would see him through. Frank, after less than two weeks in France, now found himself not only in the front line, but about to take part in an attack. While the 8th Rifle Brigade had been on rest a new weapon was moving up from Abbeville to be used for the first time: the tank. More than forty tanks had been brought forward, and would take part in what later became known as the Battle of Flers-Courcelette, when British, Canadian and New Zealand formations attacked

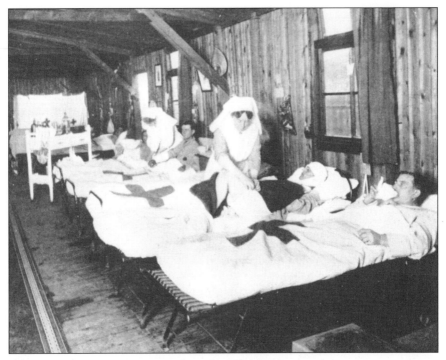

A nurse attends the wounded in a ward at a Base Hospital.

from Courcelette on the left flank to Flers in the centre, and towards Combles on the right. Frank's battalion was detailed to advance on the German positions between the villages of Ginchy and Flers. Here a track ran towards the high ground, sunken as it left Ginchy to become open as it moved towards the peak. To the west of the lane was the German position known as Pint Trench and on the high ground a long German defensive line called the Switch Trench. The 8th Rifle Brigade War Diary records what happened.

> Intense bombardment at zero 6.20am. Battalion moves forward under barrage. Very few casualties for 150 yards. Heavy losses in next 200 yards. Many Germans in Pint Trench. Pint Trench captured. Battalion reaches its objective, Switch Trench with no officers. Dig-outs bombed. Some prisoners taken. 2 machine guns captured, 1 blown up . . . Consolidation started . . . Strength of battalion in Switch Trench 6 officers and Medical Officer and 160 Other Ranks.[11]

The War Diary also includes an extensive casualty list, in which Frank's name appears showing that he had been wounded in action on 15 September. Advancing into a piece of open ground, flanked by two trench systems, the 8th Rifle Brigade has seemingly been hit by cross fire which cost them several hundred casualties, including Frank. Despite these losses the objective had been taken, and to their right the Guards had taken Ginchy, and to their left Flers was also captured. But Frank probably knew nothing of this. The War Diary also records a lack of stretcher bearers and stretchers, and how Frank was evacuated will probably never be known. The nearest medical facilities were beyond Delville Wood, and from here motor ambulances would have taken him to a Casualty Clearing Station (CCS) near Albert. A CCS was a proper medical facility occupying more than a square mile of ground, with surgeons who could perform operations, X-ray and blood transfusion facilities. Here a casualty would be stabilised, operated on if required, and then transferred to a Hospital Train and taken to a Base Hospital.

While in hospital in Rouen, Frank recovered enough to have this photograph taken. Within a few days complications set in and he died of his wounds.

The exact nature of Frank's wound is not recorded, but it is likely to have been a gun-shot wound caused by rifle or machine-gun fire, given the fact that he was advancing in the open towards an entrenched enemy. In these circumstances leg wounds were very common as the weapons were being fired from the front of the trench, the parapet, at just above ground level and hitting their targets in the lower limbs. No letters survive from Frank's time in the hospital, and sadly the admission records for Rouen were destroyed, but a single photograph survives showing him in 'Hospital Blues'. This blue uniform with a red tie was worn by soldiers convalescing, and the photograph of Frank shows him from the waist up with no obvious wounds visible, further supporting that his injury was to the legs. He looks gaunt and drawn, and quite exhausted, and the arrival of such a photograph must have been shocking to his parents. At some point on 25 September 1916 complications set in. Leg wounds could easily get infected and in a war with no antibiotics available, the chances of dying from infection were high, and Frank's short war came to an end as he died of his wounds this day; after less than four weeks at the front and a mere handful of days on the battlefield. The usual telegram announcing his day arrived at 50 Lawford Road, dealing a crushing blow to his parents and his 'best girl' Gertrude. His mother later wrote: 'from his letters to me he tried, as he always did, to save me any anxiety. I am quite resigned and can say at last 'Thy will be done'.'[12]

Francis Hansell Davies was one of more than 350,00 British casualties on the Somme in 1916. His short war from training in the spring of 1916 to his few weeks of active service is not untypical of the later part of the fighting on the Somme, and indeed would become increasingly commonplace as conscription brought young men into the Army, trained them to a basic level and pitched them straight into the front line. In a strange symmetry, nearly a century later the deaths of young riflemen like Frank are still being reported as the modern war in Afghanistan continues into its tenth year.

Researching Frank Davies

Frank Davies was one of the many thousands of soldiers whose records were lost in bombing during the Second World War. While Frank's story could to a certain degree be traced through surviving letters, postcards and photographs, and was ironically helped by the fact that he had died in the war – giving a final period to look at – what does a researcher do when all that survives is the records of a soldier's medals? The Medal Index Cards, which include all those who served overseas in the Great War, display some code in the section that relates to what medals were issued which indicates which volume and page of the actual Medal Rolls the entry for this soldier is contained in. Very few people go beyond the Medal Index Cards because they are easily available online, but the Medal Rolls in WO329 at TNA are a potential treasure trove of information. While Frank's battalion of his regiment was known because he had died, the key to unlocking where an infantry soldier fought is to ascertain his battalion. It is only rarely indicated on a Medal Index Card, but it is recorded on the Medal Rolls. If he changed battalion that is also recorded, and some Medal Rolls even include exact dates of overseas service. With the battalion ascertained, the next thing for Frank was to find out when he went overseas; as he was awarded just the British War and Victory medals this was not recorded on his Medal Index Card or on the Medal Roll. In Frank's case the date was known from his letters, but without that information one other way to work this out is to use *Soldiers Died in the Great War* in a slightly different way. The digitised CD-ROM version by Naval and Military Press (available at TNA and many major libraries) is a proper database so it can be manipulated to locate information. In this case it can be tweaked to provide a list of men from the Rifle Brigade with numbers similar to Frank's. Armed with this the list can then be put in date order. This will immediately tell you when men with these numbers first died overseas, and given survival rates in the infantry it is likely that the first man died within a month or so of arrival. Soldier's numbers in the Great War were not unique but they did normally relate to a date of enlistment, and therefore to a date that the man would be posted overseas.

Once Frank's battalion and date overseas was known the battalion War Diary in WO95 could be used to follow his movements. There is a two-volume regimental history of the Rifle Brigade, now reprinted, which can also be consulted to gain some depth of knowledge. Frank's service was largely on the Somme, and there are perhaps more books on this battle than any other of the war, so there is plenty of scope to gain some wider perspective on where he was.

When a soldier was wounded like Frank and admitted to medical facilities behind the lines his name was entered in an Admission and Discharge Book. Only a few of these survive in class MH106 at TNA, but if a medical unit is known or an area where a man was wounded is known, it is possible to work out which medical units with surviving records were located in that area and it may be possible to find an entry in one of the Admission Books. All medical units also wrote a War Diary and while these do not normally record names of those admitted, it is always worth checking them in class WO95 at TNA, but if you have no idea where a man was admitted, it could be a long search.

Notes

1. From letter dated 16 April 1916, in the author's collection.
2. From letters in the author's collection.
3. Ibid.
4. Ibid.
5. Ibid.
6. Ibid.
7. Ibid.
8. 8th Battalion Rifle Brigade War Diary TNA WO95/1895. Crown Copyright.
9. From letters in the author's collection.
10. Sarah Frances 'Fanny' Durack was born in Sydney in 1889 and in the Edwardian period became a leading Australian swimmer. By 1910 she held every swimming record possible and won a gold medal at the Stockholm Olympics in 1912 for 100m freestyle. She died in 1956 and was probably never aware of the title Australian troops gave the church in Albert.
11. 8th Battalion Rifle Brigade War Diary TNA WO95/1895. Crown Copyright.
12. Extract from parish magazine in the author's collection.

Chapter Seven

A VICAR'S SON ON THREE FRONTS

William Coburn Cowper's Long Journey from France to Palestine

The rise of the British middle classes in the Victorian period was epitomised by what can only be described as a quaint English tradition – the clergyman's family. Church and Protestant religion were at the foundation of Victorian society, and priests had been permitted to marry for some time. The local parish priest was the centre of many urban and rural communities, and was looked to as an example, both spiritually and socially. In the years before the Great War in South London, one such priest was Herbert William Cowper. Records show that he was born in Cambridge in 1862, studied theology at Cambridge University and entered the priesthood as a young man. His first marriage ended in tragedy when his wife died of complications after giving birth. Some years later he met Theresa while he was a priest in St Ives, Cornwall, and they married in 1891. They had four children: Dora, William Coburn, Leonard and Lawrence between 1893 and 1900. William Coburn Cowper, always known as Coburn in the family, was born in Wandsworth, London, in 1896. As a young man he was surrounded by a loving family, which was heavily involved in the local community. Herbert was so committed to where he lived he opted for his son to be educated locally, rather than send him off to boarding school as was often the norm. Coburn had a happy time at Highfield School in Trinity Road, Wandsworth, only a short walk from home. He did well here, was awarded a school prize in December 1910 and left with an excellent reference from his old headmaster. Like many Edwardian middle-class boys, he had no idea where his future lay, and he got a job in insurance, working for a company in the City and commuting in from Wandsworth each day.

Then in the late summer of 1914 his life, and the world, would change forever. The war would have been a great topic of conversation in the Cowper household, and brought up on duty and patriotism, Coburn was not one to shirk his responsibilities. However, he was not alone in wishing to enlist to 'do his bit' and the local units around Wandsworth were all but full in September 1914 when Lord Kitchener, Secretary of State for War, called for 100,000 volunteers. London recruiting was dominated by the London Regiment, an all Territorial Army (although it was called the Territorial Force then) regiment formed of twenty-six battalions located in communities in central and outer London. The Queen's battalions of the London Regiment, the headquarters of which were in the Clapham–Battersea area, were the obvious choice but Coburn could not find a vacancy. Instead, he travelled to Flodden Road in Camberwell where he joined the 21st Battalion London Regiment (First Surrey Rifles) as a rifleman. So great was the response that the original 21st Londons was already at full complement, so a second battalion, and soon a third battalion were formed. Coburn joined the 2/21st and immediately went into camp near Redhill.

Soon afterwards he had his first photograph taken in uniform, which he sent home to his parents in Wandsworth. It shows the young, fresh-faced Coburn in khaki. He is wearing a set of leather equipment, issued to many Territorial and Volunteer units as not enough webbing had been produced, and he proudly holds a rifle with fixed bayonet in his hands. On close inspection, the rifle is a Japanese Ariska. Not only did the War Office lack proper uniforms, had to produce leather instead of webbing gear, it also did not have enough rifles to give to all those who had joined up in 1914. Many old pattern rifles came out of stores, but even these proved insufficient, so contracts went out and the government bought thousands of these rifles from their ally, Japan. The regimental history records: 'About this time our long expected rifles arrived, packed solid in mysterious looking cases. It was the talk of the Battalion, but our feelings were of a mixed order when it was discovered that they hailed from Japan. Not a few realised more deeply than ever the inadequacy of our national resources.'[1]

A proud Coburn Cowper in full kit as a rifleman in the 2/21st London Regiment (First Surrey Rifles) at camp, 1915.

*Brother Leonard had joined the Artist's Rifles in
London and went to their training camp in Essex.*

Coburn proved to be a good soldier, and he was soon promoted to lance
corporal and then full corporal. One of his officers recognised a young man
with a good, middle-class background and enquired as to why he had not
sought a commission as an officer? It is likely, given the self-effacing nature
of the Cowper family, that it hadn't even occurred to him. But encouraged
to pursue it, he applied and was accepted, and gazetted a second lieutenant
in the First Surrey Rifles on 24 December 1915. Officer training with the
3/21st followed, and he soon returned to the 2/21st as a platoon
commander.

After nearly two years in training, Coburn and his comrades in the
2/21st were finally going to France. No record of his own thoughts exist for
that time, but as the first Cowper son to go on active service we can only
but wonder at the anxiousness of his parents. His father, as a parish priest,
had visited many families in Wandsworth who had lost someone. Would
the same fate await him and his close little family? The regimental history,
however, records that those in the unit felt nothing but jubilation: 'At
length . . . after nearly two years in England, the minute of departure came.

Coburn Cowper (middle row, third from left) photographed with men of his platoon, 1915.

Collecting loaves for the battalion in the local town, Coburn is standing on the tailgate of the wagon.

Now a commissioned officer in the 2/21st Londons, Coburn in France with his full 'trench kit', 1916.

The Battalion was launched . . . And, by gad! the train really is moving out of Warminster Station. Jump in, you officers! We are off to France!'[2]

As a platoon officer, Coburn's platoon of more than forty men would have travelled together in the trains, the transport and along the roads allocated to the battalion. After some time at a base camp close to the port of Le Havre, where they unloaded, they moved up nearer to the front at the village of Louez. While the journey via Rouen had been by train, the last lap was on foot along the dead straight Roman roads of Northern France. It was a taxing march, but suddenly the war was with them.

> There was a general unspoken wonder as to what would happen if a shell dropped . . . when a tremendous explosion took place and a great flare shot up into the sky. Then that moment followed, afterwards so familiar, when one wonders if one is wounded, and when the pain will begin. It passed, and the men started whistling. It turned out that the explosion had come from a heavy howitzer that fired once an hour during the night from the other side of a hedge on our left. Our training had not even prepared us for that. We felt a little more confident. We were no longer green.[3]

With a glimpse into the war, the men of Coburn's battalion found themselves sent immediately to the trenches around the village of Ecuire, close to the city of Arras. Here they were attached to experienced troops of the 51st (Highland) Division for instruction, and slowly they settled into the routine of a so-called 'quiet' sector. Coburn's notebook gives an insight into the daily routine: 'Stand to from 6.45am – about ¾ hour. Breakfast 8 o'clock. Washing 9am. Everybody to be washed and shaved by 10.30. Carry out fatigues. Dinner 1 o'clock. Tea 5 o'clock. Stand to evening – 5.45. Evening; latrines to be dug, inspect rifles and Iron Rations.'[4] Coburn himself was particularly well equipped for the trenches. A contemporary photograph shows him in full trench kit, with newly issued gas mask and helmet. One of his fellow officers, who would figure heavily throughout his life, Rowlands Coldicott, later wrote:

> I like to imagine him as he used to appear in France when going on duty, at the entrance to my dug-out, very much dressed for the part, armed at all points, clad in a voluminous and skirty trench-coat which bulged and overflowed his equipment, and seemingly hung all over with murderous weapons. Above it a fresh boyish countenance, shyly conscious of the fun it was creating, told that war was an unpleasant tonic that had to be swallowed somehow.[5]

Leonard had been commissioned into the Northumberland Fusiliers, and after only a few weeks at the front was killed in November 1916, just as Coburn was heading for Salonika.

While Coburn was in the trenches at Vimy Ridge in late July, he received a short note from his sister Dora informing him that Leonard was now on active service. His training as an officer had come to an end, and Leonard had proceeded to the Infantry Base Depot at Rouen. The depot was full of news of the heavy losses on the Somme, and his own regiment, the Northumberland Fusiliers, had suffered heavily in the fighting at La Boisselle a few weeks before when the Tyneside Irish and Scottish battalions had all but been wiped out on the first day of the battle. Gradually, they were being brought up to strength, and Leonard was posted as a reenforcement to the 20th (1st Tyneside Scottish) Battalion, and he joined them in the trenches on the Somme just as they were pulling out and heading north to a 'quiet' sector. While Leonard was no doubt pleased to be joining his brother on the battlefield, for now taking part in a big operation was unlikely and his unit would be concerned with the day-to-day activities of trench warfare in the meantime.

Coburn meanwhile continued to live a very similar life. His battalion, and indeed the entire 60th (London) Division, of which they were a part, could hear the rumble of the bombardments to the south and all wondered whether they would take part in the Battle of the Somme. The regimental historian later recorded: 'It was now generally accepted that we were destined for the Somme, and a new spirit of seriousness spread over the Battalion . . . The general sentiment ran that if we were to be decimated – and all knew what the Somme would have in store – we might at least die decently, and put up a good last show.'[6]

But their destiny did not lie in the fields of Picardy. Unbeknown to Coburn and his comrades in the 2/21st they were in fact en route to an entirely new theatre of war. In early November they were out on rest when orders arrived. Many presumed it was the inevitable instructions for the Somme but in fact:

> the astonishing news was circulated that we were to be diverted to Salonika for the Macedonia front. The news came at the last moment . . . Mixed feelings now reigned in the battalion, but for the most part it was expected that we were going to have a very good time, and Salonika was popularly pictured as a city of white palaces where there were dancing halls and Chinese lanterns . . . where everyone including the soldiery, lived a life of relaxation and careless gaiety . . . the short life with the glorious end was evidentially not for this unit. Destiny had not done with us yet, she was only beginning to show her hand.[7]

For most men the mention of the word Salonika caused some confusion, and even Coburn with a good education probably would have struggled to find it on the map. Although British troops had actually been in the country since late 1915, the biggest build up to date was in 1916 as troops were transferred in from Egypt and France. The enemy here was not Germany, but Bulgaria, allied to Germany and Austro-Hungary, and the borders of which touched on the battle zone. In many ways the Balkans had laid the seeds for the Great War, and now Britain was here to ensure their Greek

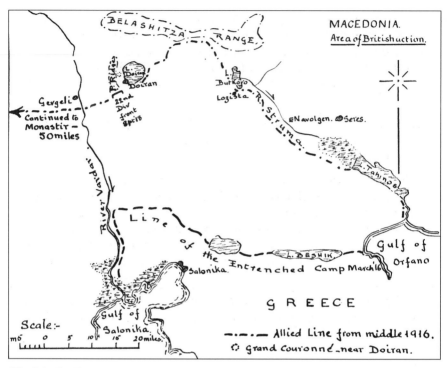

The Salonika Front, 1916.

allies were not overrun. But as Coburn reached Salonika news came from home, the worst possible news – Leonard was dead. He had been killed in a 'quiet sector' on 7 November 1916, as Coburn had been en route. An explosion of a trench mortar shell close to his dugout had killed him outright. One of his fellow officers, George Riding, later wrote,

> we came from the same battalion, and crossed together. At the Base we shared a tent, our first billet here in this little French village was in a garret together, and our lives ran together until he was called to his new battalion. We became the very closest of friends . . . I am many years older than he was, and a schoolmaster, and his open-hearted boyhood soon won its way, as it has with all who knew him. At all sorts of times he would say: 'I can just picture them all at home!' He used to tell me . . . of how he loved going to Church to hear the pater preach, of his sister and the jolly times they had together . . .

We here are all genuinely sorry, officers and men alike, and yesterday I went among the French villagers here, in the shops where we had laughed and joked together over his attempts to talk with them in the farms and houses. All knew him and showed the deepest sorrow – 'the fair young officer who was always smiling' was the way they described him.[8]

Coburn's parents took the news badly, as did the whole, very close family. But even a few weeks later, Herbert Cowper wrote to his son in a typical cheerful manner,

It is so wonderful to think of you seeing so much of the world and having such marvellous experiences while you are still so young. What a man it must be making of you! And what an astonishing person you will be to us all when, please God, you come home to tell the tale of your travels and adventures. How we long for the day of your return! We do indeed hope the war will be over soon.[9]

But the end of the war was a long way off, and for Coburn and his comrades on the front line in Salonika, a new regime began. The front was pretty quiet at this time, and winter in Macedonia was somewhat unforgiving. Heavy

Salonika, 1916.

rain filled the trenches, many of which were not much more than outposts. The roads turned into a mire of mud, and equipment, supplies and ammunition was moved up by mule, often over rough ground. The lack of infrastructure was a shock to a battalion that had experienced the permanency of France. From their front line the Bulgarian border could be seen with snow-capped mountains and pine forests. Many veterans of this campaign later complained that the weather here was the greatest enemy, and during their first few months in the line, the 2/21st had its fair share of casualties as result of the physical conditions, as much as from enemy action.

After a long period of snow, Coburn and his battalion moved into the Vardar Valley. Here the war took an even stranger twist: 'The one curious fact about our trenches that stands out is that they were almost uninhabited by day. The reason for this was that portions of them were in full view of the enemy, partly because it had not been possible to blast them deep enough in the rock.'[10] This meant that they were perched on a slope for most of the daylight hours, clinging to the soft ground in range of the enemy, but because of the angle of the contours it was almost impossible for their artillery to reach them. But reach them one day they did, and the shells contained a weapon so far rarely encountered – gas. Diphosgene gas fell on the battalion, and the new Box Respirators were quickly found and used to good effect; but it made life even more uncomfortable.

As spring came, and the weather changed for the better, hinting at the sapping heat that was the other extreme of life in Salonika, orders arrived for yet another move. As far as the War Office was concerned, Salonika was a quiet front for now, but the war against Ottoman Turkey was heating up again in Palestine, as heavy fighting in Gaza in March and April 1917 had shown. More troops were needed, and a number of formations selected and despatched to Egypt. Coburn and the 2/21st were now to make their final move of the war, and on 16 June they embarked on two transport ships for Alexandria: 'And so we bade farewell to a front where the chief enemy was the climate, and our chief experiences the joys and sorrows of a gipsy life.'[11]

Palestine was a very different theatre of war; in fact it was just that – a war, in a way that France and Salonika had not been for men of the 60th (London) Division. This is where they would win their reputation, and where the majority of their casualties suffered and battle honours won. Palestine pre-war had been part of the Ottoman Empire, and by the summer of 1917 the campaign was not going well for the British. They had been

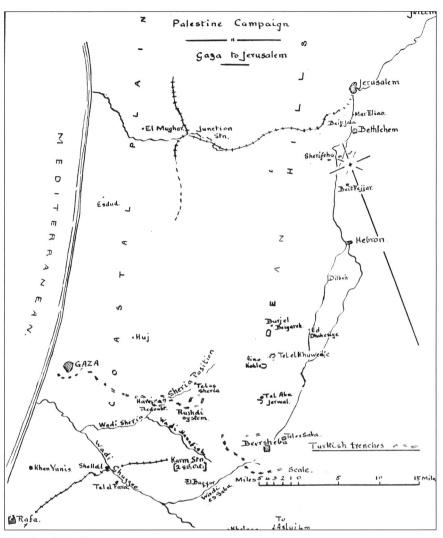

Palestine, 1917–18.

gradually pushing the Turks out of Sinai, with the eventual aim of taking Palestine completely and cutting off Turkish troops in Mesopotamia, where the British were engaged against them simultaneously. Fighting in Gaza had ended in stalemate, with huge losses and a change of command. As the London men moved in, so did a new Commander in Chief, Edmund

Allenby. Allenby would prove a fine desert commander, whose achievements are largely unknown more than ninety years later. Re-organising his forces, Allenby went on the offensive in October 1917 and the 2/21st was to be heavily involved. Several months in the hot desert had seen the battalion acclimatise to life in Palestine, and Coburn now found himself in charge of the battalion's Lewis machine guns. These American-designed weapons were now the automatic fire support for all infantry battalions, and their role became increasingly important. The regimental history recorded:

> now, too, the Lewis gunners (under Lieut. Cowper) were trained again and brought into prominence. These still depended on mules for their transport . . . Officers still rode their horses. We wore but little. A shirt, open at the neck and with sleeves rolled up, a pair of scanty 'shorts', a pair of puttees ending at the bare knee. A sun helmet – this completed out attire.[12]

By October the battalion was committed to the new operations, as it took over ground at Tel El Fara and advanced eastwards in a night attack on Beersheba. The main battle there was fought by the mounted units under Allenby's command, including Australian, British and New Zealand

In the scrub of Palestine in the Jordan Valley, Coburn Cowper (front left) is seen with other officers of his battalion, including Colonel Jervois (centre).

Coburn Cowper (right) is seen with a colleague, Captain Walter, in Jerusalem, not long before the disbandment of 2/21st Londons, January 1918.

cavalry. The Londons approached it from the Wadi El Saba from the west, and stormed a hill at bayonet point supported by Cowper's Lewis guns. A dust storm enveloped the battlefields as October gave way to November, but it had been a victory and the route now lay open to Jerusalem. If that fell, then the outcome of operations in Palestine would be a foregone conclusion.

By early December 1917 Coburn and his Lewis gunners were with the battalion in the foot hills close to Jerusalem. On the 7th the British troops attacked in the pouring rain and took the Turkish defenders by surprise; an irony that success should come in such poor weather when most of the campaign had been fought in the sweltering heat. Crossing the brow of a hill, the battalion was met with a magnificent view of the city of Jerusalem, and the final fighting took them into the streets where, the regimental history recorded, they were 'hemmed in on both sides by sightseers, like troops in a London crowd'.[13] Jerusalem fell, and the men of the 60th (London) Division, Coburn among them, took part in a triumphant march as liberators of this most famous of cities, with their commander General Allenby at their head.

The last year of the conflict in Palestine saw Coburn promoted to the rank of captain and in early 1918 he became adjutant of the 2/21st. This new position was essentially a desk job, where he compiled the daily War Diary, and kept the paper trail that re-supplied and re-equipped the battalion in order. But the days of the 2/21st were numbered. In 1918 the British Army was suffering a manpower problem; conscription, successful as it was, was unable to provide enough men to garrison all the battalions on active service. In Palestine the units would be bolstered by the arrival of Indian army regiments, and the number of British Army battalions would be reduced so that a degree of full strength could be maintained as a whole. In June 1918 the battalion was therefore cut into the three, with the majority – Coburn among them – being sent to the 2/22nd Battalion London Regiment (Queen's). The regimental history recorded:

> To most of us this order was a tragedy, for the Battalion was our other home. Many of the men had been with it since the beginning of the war. A great depression fell upon everyone. It was hard luck that we should have travelled so far and for so long and not be permitted to survive as an entity until the end.[14]

Within a few months, when the campaign in Palestine went into its final phase as the Turks were gradually routed, Coburn was transferred to the

*After three years of active service, a weary Coburn
Cowper in Palestine while acting as brigade major, 1919.*

staff of the 181st Infantry Brigade, which his new and former battalion had
been a part. His skill at paperwork, no doubt learnt as an insurance clerk,
had proved so good he was promoted. Coburn had swapped the sword for
the pen, and would remain in his post well beyond the end of the war in
Palestine, which concluded in October 1918. He remained in theatre for
another year, assisting with the establishment of the British regime in
Palestine and aiding in the demobilisation of men from the 60th (London)
Division. He at last came home to his parents in Wandsworth in the autumn
of 1919. Coburn's final photograph prior to demobilisation shows a tired
face – worn out by four years of warfare and experiences on three different
battlefronts.

In the years immediately following the war Coburn returned to his job as
an insurance clerk in London. Like many young men of his generation he
found it difficult to settle down; life as a city worker seemed too normal
after the war, and many of Coburn's co-workers were younger men who

War over, and life renews – Coburn Cowper with his parents on his wedding day in 1924.

hadn't served. His father remained a local parish priest, and his mother very active in the local community. Having lost Leonard in 1916, they were both heavily involved in the project for a local Wandsworth war memorial. In the early 1920s Coburn met Gertrude Rolls and fell in love; they married at her local church in Banstead in July 1924. About the same time an old Army friend, Rowlands Coldicott, got in touch with Coburn. Coldicott was establishing a new seaside village at Middleton-on-Sea, and was anxious to get Coburn involved. They went into business together, and by this time Coburn and his wife were living in Sussex. Coldicott never really achieved his vision, and the stock-market crashes no doubt affected investors, but Coburn would remain on the south coast for the rest of his life. Following the death of his mother, Coburn's father retired from church life in London and moved to live close to him in Sussex, becoming local priest at Aldwick, near Bognor, until his death in 1932. With the outbreak of the Second World War, Coburn was back in uniform with the Sussex Home Guard. He subsequently retired to Worthing, where he passed away in the summer of

1986, seventy years after the young south London vicar's son had marched off to a war on three fronts.

Researching William Coburn Cowper

Researching officers who served in the Great War is generally somewhat easier than ordinary soldiers. There is a much higher survival rate for service papers, and many contemporary records mention officers by name. However, for William Coburn Cowper, his later post-war service means that his records are still with the Ministry of Defence, so to trace his war and movements it required looking at a number of sources rather than just the normal quicker route of accessing service papers. The one benefit in Cowper's case was that a large collection of documentation survived relating to his war service, the sort of documents many families have, and which were invaluable for ascertaining the outline of his war.

To fill in the gaps, as with all members of the Army, the starting point was the Medal Index Cards. These showed which unit he served with, 2/21st Battalion London Regiment, and that he rose to the rank of acting captain. Using the Monthly Army Lists, published by the War Office and now available in the library at TNA or at the National Army Museum, the dates of his commission and promotions could be charted. Knowing which unit he was with meant that the War Diaries for his battalion in France, Salonika and Palestine could be accessed, and this enabled a detailed picture of where he served and what the unit was doing to be constructed. This was further supplemented by checking regimental history bibliographies to discover his regiment had a published war history. This added a great deal of further detail, giving insight into the sort of things Cowper would have seen and experienced, and the anecdotes about what the unit was doing made the story of his war seem more real. His main theatre of war was Palestine, and checking bibliographies and online library indexes for this subject resulted in the discovery of a book covering the London battalion on this front. An added bonus was that it was written by Cowper's lifelong friend, and he was frequently mentioned in it. The British 'Official History' also proved a useful source, especially the map volumes, which are now available in a digital form. His post-war life was tracked via Ancestry, but his involvement with Middleton-on-Sea linked him into a number of sources about contemporary architecture and local history for this area.

Notes

1. Anon., *A War Record of the 21st London Regiment (First Surrey Rifles) 1914–1919* (H.B. Skinner & Co., 1927), p. 136.
2. Ibid., p. 145.
3. Ibid., p. 147.
4. Papers in the author's collection.
5. R. Coldicott, *London Men In Palestine* (Edward Arnold, 1919), p. 66.
6. Anon., *A War Record of the 21st London Regiment*, p. 161.
7. Ibid., p. 162.
8. Papers in the author's collection.
9. Ibid.
10. Anon., *A War Record of the 21st London Regiment*, p. 181.
11. Ibid., p. 185.
12. Ibid., p. 189.
13. Ibid., p. 207.
14. Ibid., p. 218.

Chapter Eight

I DIED IN HELL . . . THEY CALLED IT PASSCHENDAELE

Henry Joseph Penn, a Royal Marine in France and Flanders

Even at the outbreak of war in August 1914 the Royal Marines had a proud tradition of service for Britain and the Empire. The Navy's requirement for ground troops was as old as ships had been at sea, and this was how the Royal Marines had come into being; as a military arm of the Navy that could be used to board ships at sea, defend vessels and make armed landing parties. While the early twentieth century had seen massive developments in ship technology, there was still a requirement for Marines but the world situation was changing and the role Marines would take was also changing. The idea of a Marine Brigade to be committed to an overseas battlefield, most likely Europe, had been muted several years before the war, and to talk of 'Royal Marines' is perhaps a little misleading as at the outbreak of war there were three branches: Royal Marine Light Infantry, Royal Marine Artillery and Royal Marines Band. These three branches totalled more than 18,000 personnel in 1914 alone,[1] and were dominated by the Royal Marine Light Infantry, which would be become the main source of ground troops during the war. When a Marine enlisted he was posted to a home depot at one of the ports such as Chatham, Deal, Portsmouth and Plymouth. Here he would undergo training, which is described below in 1915:

On entering the Barracks one is struck by the mere atmosphere of the place in which these men are trained; outside the barrack gate are jerry-built houses, little shops, & all that one would expect in this suburb of a naval town; inside is cleanliness, solidity & neat efficiency, – one passes into a world that is better ordered, better managed, & of more healthy atmosphere than the civilian world outside. From the magnificent mess room of the officers' mess to the great central kitchen in which the men's meals are prepared, one gathers a sense of things done in the best possible way, & that sense persists in surveying the training of the men, the provisions for their comfort, the range of sport & recreation provided for their spare time – for every detail of their lives in the period of training. From this period they pass equipped, mentally & physically, to take their places in the ships of the Fleet, with the Armies in France & the Dardanelles, in German South-West Africa, or on anti-aircraft service in the United Kingdom.[2]

In the early stages of the war, the Royal Marine Brigade formed of units from the Port Depots had served with the newly formed Royal Naval Division in Belgium. The men had worn a combination of khaki and naval blue uniforms, and a wide mix of weapons and equipment. Many of the men had been older reservists, and had struggled to cope with long marches on the cobbled roads of Flanders. By no means a failure, it was clear that a new approach to the use, equipping and manning within the Royal Marine Light Infantry would be needed. This was partially addressed by the time they fought at Gallipoli in 1915, and while the Corps fought and suffered casualties, they would need to replace them with new recruits, so from August 1914 the Royal Marines had actively sought volunteers in the same way as the Army. In 1914, therefore, a system of 'short service' was brought in whereby men could chose to enlist for the duration of the war, rather than a set period as had previously been the case. With a massive influx of men, as happened in 1914 and 1915, the training system had to be simplified, and many men had less than six weeks of training before being posted to a unit. During the Gallipoli campaign the Depot units were disbanded and the 1st and 2nd Battalions Royal Marine Light Infantry formed in their place, remaining with the Royal Naval Division for much of the rest of the war.

Henry Joseph Penn was a young Londoner who joined the Royal Marine Light Infantry in 1915, at a point when voluntary enlistment was changing. Henry was only 17 years and 11 months when he joined up in London on

Henry Joseph Penn, photographed on leave just prior to departing for France, April 1917.

29 December 1915. At this time the Lord Derby Scheme, the final chance to enlist voluntarily, was coming to an end. Although he was under age, it appears he did not want to wait until he was 18 and would be compulsorily enlisted under the proposed system of conscription that was going to be introduced in 1916. His background, despite his young age, was at sea; he listed his trade as 'Seaman' on his enlistment papers. His house in Pearcroft Road, Leytonstone, was a long way from the sea, but only a tram's journey from the docks in London along the Thames, where he is likely to have worked since leaving school. Before the Great War the Thames and its associated industries were one of the greatest employers in the city. Having joined the Royal Marines, he was posted to the Deal Depot in Kent for training. Unlike many volunteers who had lied about his age, Henry had been upfront and told the recruiting sergeant. They had accepted him, but his actual service would not officially start until he was 18, some twenty-nine days after he joined up. In Deal he would have been taught the basics of Royal Marine service, and given instruction on drill, discipline, bayonet fighting and musketry – firing his rifle. By the time his training was over the Royal Naval Division, containing the two Royal Marine battalions, had arrived in France from Egypt, where they had been since the end of the Gallipoli campaign. At this point they had no need for a great deal of re-enforcements, so Henry found himself held back at the

Royal Marines in training.

Depot in Deal. In the summer of 1916 he was transferred to Chatham, and joined the Depot there.

Finally, after the costly fighting on the Somme in November 1916, and the operations along the Ancre Valley where the Royal Marines lost further men in February 1917, he was needed. He went with a draft to France on 14 April 1917 where he was posted to the 1st Battalion Royal Marine Light Infantry. However, like all those arriving on the Western Front at this time, it wasn't an immediate transfer. On arrival in France drafts like the one Henry was with were posted to an Infantry Base Depot at Etaples for further training. Here Henry and the men with him would have been issued with gas masks, by now the new Small Box Respirators, the first proper gas masks issued to British troops, and also received the training to go with them. There were also long days in the 'Bull Ring', the large training ground on the dunes at Etaples where further drill and bayonet fighting were taught. Their time here at an end, more than two weeks had passed and they were loaded on a troop train at Etaples station and made their way towards the front. The 1st Royal Marines' War Diary shows that while they were finishing their training the battalion was involved in bitter fighting at Arras. At this point a draft of more than a hundred re-enforcements joined at the village of Frévillers, north-west of Arras, where the unit was out on rest after the recent operations. While no doubt expecting to go straight into battle, Henry found himself on labouring duties, digging trenches, carrying out wiring and fixing up barbed wire defences in the reserve lines closer to Arras. At the end of the month they got near to the front line and a few days later took over the trenches at Gavrelle. This village had been where the Marines had fought in April, and captured the high ground around the Gavrelle Windmill. This now gave them the advantage of height, and several local counterattacks by the Germans to regain the ground had all ended in failure. The weather had taken a turn for the worse with heavy rain, and the War Diary records that the trenches were 'in very bad state'.[3] The men spent most of their time repairing them rather than fighting the enemy, and over the course of the summer as the battalion carried out what the War Diary called 'usual trench routine' it is quite likely Henry never once had the opportunity to fire his rifle, and almost certainly never saw a German at this time. It certainly must have appeared to be a very odd war, and in great contrast to the propaganda in the newspapers and in the cinemas back home. However, while this period had largely seen Henry's battalion, and indeed the entire division, work on the infrastructure of the ground around Gavrelle that they had captured in the Battle of Arras, unbeknown to them, the following spring the well-prepared trench lines, firing positions and dugouts would be a contributing factor in this ground holding out against the German offensive of March 1918. As summer moved into autumn, the rain continued and made life around Gavrelle difficult, but in the first few days of October orders arrived dictating a change of sector. The battalion was on the move to Ypres, and the Battle of Passchendaele.

The shattered battlefield at Passchendaele.

All summer the Royal Naval Division had been aware of the operations taking place in Flanders. This had started with the explosion of the nineteen Messines mines in June 1917, the shock wave of which had been felt at Gavrelle more than 30 miles to the south. Units coming through Arras over the next few months reported on the next phase of the battle. From 31 July the British began to advance from positions north-east of Ypres, with the objective of advancing on Passchendaele village and the Passchendaele Ridge, and effecting a breakout to sweep north to the coast and overrun German submarine bases, causing great problems to allied shipping. The attack had initially gone well, but on the evening of the first day, 31 July, it had started to rain and hardly stopped since. Tremendous bombardments which smashed all the drainage systems and turned the battlefield into a lunar landscape of shell hole, combined with heavy rainfall, made this arguably the most horrific battlefield on which British soldiers fought during the Great War. War poet Siegfried Sassoon later wrote,

I died in Hell
(they called it Passchendaele) my wound was slight
and I was hobbling back; and then a shell
burst slick upon the duckboards; so I fell
into the bottomless mud, and lost the light.[4]

Indeed, legend was that the glutinous mud of Flanders would swallow men up, and certainly the records of that time show not only huge numbers of missing soldiers, but tanks and field guns sinking into the mud too.

Flanders mud had become proverbial, and even under ordinary conditions exposed the troops in the front system to exceptional hardships. Front line and communication trenches were non-existent. The forward system consisted of posts isolated from each other by a sea of mud, and the support line of another line of posts, the elements of a trench, or more probably, of a ruined farmhouse and outbuildings where a company or so could be concentrated . . . The enemy posts lay often between our own, and every ration and water party had to be prepared to fight its way forward . . . All supplies and reinforcements had to be brought up on duckboard tracks, which with every advance stretched further and further forward. Off these tracks progress was impossible, yet the reliance placed on them was an evil necessity . . . To turn aside by so much as a yard was to plunge waist-deep in a sea of mud, where the bodies of the dead were rotting unburied as in the primeval slime.[5]

It was this nightmare scene that the young ex-seaman from Leytonstone, Henry Penn, found himself in during October 1917. His battalion had moved by train from Arras to near Poperinghe, and gone into camp close by in a large wooded area east of the town, known as Dirty Bucket Camp. Dirty it indeed was in October 1917, but its name came from an old Flemish pub close by whose translated name was 'Dirty Bucket Estaminet'. There were huts there, and from the woods a specially constructed plank road headed out to the front beyond Ypres. Thinking that was the route for them, the 1st

Royal Marines instead marched back across the border of Belgium into France to the village of Wormhoudt to a training area where they practised the attack. The final phase of the Battle of Passchendaele was approaching, and the Royal Naval Division was attached to the Canadian Corps for the assault on the ground leading to Passchendaele village. 'Training behind the line, learning from carefully constructed models the supposed location of every enemy post and trench on their prospective front, the 188th Brigade [of which 1st Royal Marines was a part] was looking forward with confidence to the impending battle.'[6]

With this training over they returned to Ypres by 'Old Bill Bus'. These were former London buses, of the type Henry had no doubt used as a young man. On their arrival in France in 1914 they had initially retained their red London colours but were now painted green, with all the windows boarded up. Debussing in the area of the Yser Canal, north of the city, from here they could see that the rising ground beyond gave way to the front-line areas and the ground around Passchendaele. From here they marched across the smashed ground, using the labyrinth of duckboard tracks, which took Henry and his comrades to the village of Poelcapelle, identifiable as a village simply by the colour of the mud, which showed traces of brick dust and stone, and a large mound where the church had been. Just east of the village was a small collection of farm buildings around a position marked on the maps as Oxford House. It was from here that the attack would made, with the Canadians on the right.

> The chief tactical features on the intended front of attack were the Paddebeek, a flooded streamlet running parallel to our front at a distance of some five hundred yards to the right front . . . This side of the Paddebeek the main enemy posts were believed to be in five groups of ruins and pill boxes known as Berks Houses, Bray Farm, Banff House, Sourd Farm and Varlet Farm, and an isolated trench, near our junction with the Canadians, known as Source Trench.[7]

Most of the German defences were built around these farms or a series of fortified shell holes. There had previously been several attacks here involving both British and New Zealand troops, with little success. The bodies of many of those who had fallen in these actions still littered the ground around Oxford Houses, gradually becoming part of the battlefield. It had been decided to occupy the positions overlooking the ground to be assaulted a full day in advance, giving the attacking battalions time to become acquainted with a landscape with so few obvious landmarks. But,

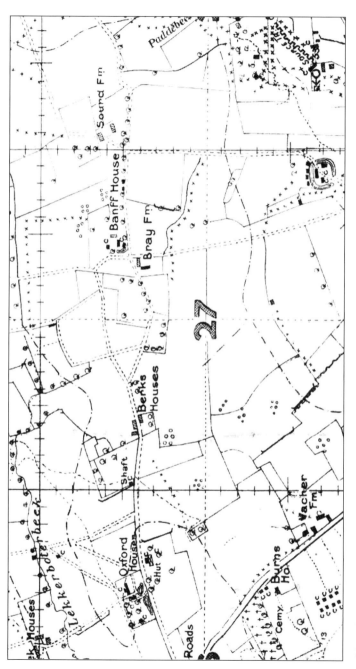

Map of the Varlet Farm battlefield, where Henry Penn died. (Dave O'Mara)

the historian of the Royal Naval Division felt this was a mistake: 'The time was, of course, too short, but this was only another instance of the impossibility of the conditions; no troops could stay longer in the line and still be fit for an advance.'[8]

The 1st Royal Marines were on the left of the advance, and detailed to attack and take Berks Houses, Bray Farm and Banff House. On the eve of the battle they numbered 16 officers and 597 men, and as such were more than 40 per cent below full strength. At 5.45 am on 26 October 1917 the advance began, in heavy rain. Henry was finally in action, and despite all the weather problems and the physical conditions on the battlefield, his battalion did well. The bombardment on their line of advance had been effective and the positions up to Bray Farm and Banff House were taken by 7.20 am. To the south the Anson Battalion of the Royal Naval Division had captured Varlet Farm. The next leap forward was across the Paddebeek beyond these locations to a farm building on the rising ground called Tournant Farm. This attack proved less successful. 'The enemy machine-gun fire from across the Paddebeek was extremely severe, and almost all the Company Commanders of the attacking battalions had become casualties. They were but small parties who had reached such of the enemy posts as had fallen, and there were other posts . . . which we had never reached.'[9]

For most of the 1st Royal Marines the battle was over. One Marine officer observed the ground close to the Paddebeek and reported back to headquarters: 'It is reported that great numbers were killed in attempting to cross the stream, and that numerous bodies of men . . . were lying along the line of it'.[10] One of those men along the banks of the Paddebeek was likely to have been Henry Joseph Penn. His exact fate was never recorded, save that he was posted missing following the fighting on 26 October 1917. Casualties in his battalion had been relatively light until after the three farmsteads had been captured, and most of their losses were sustained around the Paddebeek. Little or no information came back to his parents in Leytonstone, and no obituary appeared in the local papers with the usual letters from comrades, perhaps indicating that no one who knew survived. Henry's body was never found; like many on that deadly day of 26 October he had disappeared into the mud. Passchendaele had claimed another victim, and the state of the battlefield in that final stage of the push for the village meant that very few were buried, except by later shell fire. Few men wanted to risk their own lives to bury the dead. Nearly a century later the battlefield of Passchendaele is still giving up its secrets. All round Varlet Farm, where the Royal Naval Division fought that day, relics of the battle from shell fragments to machine guns have been found, and not far away just beyond the Paddebeek the bodies of men who fell there in 1917. The legacy of that battle, which is a byword for the sacrifice and tragedy of the Great War, lives on.

Researching Henry Joseph Penn

Although Henry Penn served with the Royal Naval Division, as a Royal Marine his records were not in the same document class as those for Fred Stoneham, described in Chapter Three. Royal Marines records consist of huge bound ledgers with a page for every recruit recording their personal details and then a chronological listing of their postings and service. Prior to the Great War most postings were to the Depot of their home port for training and then to a ship. Men of the Royal Marine Light Infantry were sent to one of the home-port battalions formed in 1914, and from 1915 in one of the two Royal Marine Light Infantry battalions which served in the Royal Naval Division. The service records are found in ADM159 at TNA and are organised by home-port prefix (PO for Portsmouth, for example) and service number. These were microfilmed and are also digitised, and can be downloaded via the Documents Online site. If a marine had a long period of service sometimes his record continues on to another page; this is normally noted at the bottom of the entry for him. These records, unlike ones for the Army, were not affected by Second World War bombing and are complete.

Henry's brief service on the Western Front, sadly not untypically brief for the last years of the war, was traced using the Royal Marine War Diaries in WO95 at TNA. These original documents are in class WO95 for the period they were on the Western Front; earlier marine diaries are in ADM137. The diaries show the day-to-day movements and activities that Henry Penn took part in, and for a wider perspective on what was going on Douglas Jerrold's history of the Royal Naval Division was useful.

During the war Royal Marine training platoons were routinely photographed by commercial photographers at the end of the training period, and copies sold to the recruits. While there is no central archive for them, the Royal Marines Museum at Eastney is worth contacting to see if they have any for the period that a marine trained in England. Sadly few are named.

Passchendaele is another iconic and much written about battle of the Great War. Lyn MacDonald's *They Called it Passchendaele* gives some glimpse into the horror of the campaign through the words of many veterans, and Peter Barton's *Passchendaele: Unseen Panoramas of the Third Battle of Ypres* gives a unique visual insight into conditions on the battlefield in 1917. Like many who fell in October 1917, Henry Penn is commemorated on the Tyne Cot Memorial, which stands on the battlefield at Passchendaele. The number of names of men from the Royal Naval Division is quite staggering. A short walk away is Varlet Farm, on the battlefield where he died. Follow-up visits to the actual ground are an important part of research into any Great War life, and a trip to the farm is well worthwhile. Aside from offering accommodation to visitors, the owners have established a small visitor centre with relics found on the ground, including one of the German machine guns that caused such havoc to the marines on the Paddebeek. The fields here are quiet now, and have returned to farming, but such a visit is rewarding when one realises how many of Penn's comrades remain unburied in this corner of hell.

Notes

1. Figure quoted at: www.jackclegg.com; accessed 1 March 2010, a useful source of Royal Marine information.
2. E.C. Vivian, 'Royal Marines – A Corps of Great Traditions' from the *Mexborough & Swinton Times*, 21 August 1915, quoted at: www.jackclegg.com; accessed 1 March 2010.
3. 1st Battalion Royal Marine Light Infantry War Diary TNA WO95/3110. Crown Copyright.
4. S. Sassoon, 'Memorial Tablet', *The War Poems of Siegfried Sassoon* (Heinemann, 1919), p. 90.
5. D. Jerrold, *The Royal Naval Division* (Hutchinson, 1927), pp. 250–1.
6. Ibid., p. 251.
7. Ibid., p. 252.
8. Ibid.
9. Ibid., p. 253.
10. Report to the 188th Brigade Headquarters TNA WO95/3108. Crown Copyright.

Chapter Nine

A GREAT WAR GUINEA PIG
Frank Plumb, Suffolk Regiment

The subject and discussion of casualties in the Great War normally conjures up images of the 'Glorious Dead'. Indeed, the phrase 'casualties' is usually considered a byword for the dead alone. This misleading use of the word has given a false image of the war, making the casual reader believe that the majority of those who served died. The reality of the Great War was that the majority of men who served survived, and the majority of 'casualties' were those who were wounded, injured and sick rather than died. One recent author who specialises in the study of soldiers with facial injuries referred to them as the 'forgotten men' of the Great War. Forgotten they may be, but they were certainly legion in terms of their numbers. Official casualty figures show that more than 5½ million servicemen became casualties on the Western Front alone during the Great War.[1] Of these nearly 2 million were battle-related casualties, and one person in that huge statistic was Frank Plumb.

Frank Plumb was born in 1897 in the small Suffolk village of Copdock, near Ipswich, where his parents ran the village Post Office. Educated at the village school, he was only 17 when the war broke out and a few months later in October 1914 he joined the 6th Cyclist Battalion of the Suffolk Regiment at Ipswich. Cyclist battalions were Territorial Force (today the Territorial Army) units formed before the war to provide infantry units equipped with bicycles for extra mobility. Their history went back to the nineteenth century and some had been employed in the Boer War. The unit

Frank Plumb (left) photographed with his brother, on home leave in 1917.

Frank joined was local to Ipswich and had attracted so many recruits that a second battalion of cyclists had been formed, called the 2/6th Battalion Suffolk Regiment. It was this unit that he was posted to, and went with them to Louth in Lincolnshire on home defence along the coast. He later recalled:

> When I originally joined the army I had joined from an advertisement in the East Anglian Daily Times calling for lads of eighteen urgently wanted to form a second battalion of the 6th Suffolk Cyclists for coast defence. This was October 1914. I went with two mates and joined that, and we went up to Lincolnshire. Within six months we were issued with Japanese carbines, live ammunition and were patrolling the coast. Then in 1915 they wanted to send us to France but they couldn't take us to France unless we volunteered again and they asked all of us if

we'd volunteer for Imperial Service. If we did we were given a badge, given home leave and then out to France in early 1916.[2]

Shortly after his eighteenth birthday Frank agreed to be sent overseas if required, but it would be many months before he was needed. The Battle of the Somme began on 1 July 1916, and on this day in front of the village of La Boiselle the 11th Battalion Suffolk Regiment took part in a disastrous attack which cost them significant casualties. Immediate replacements were required, and drafts were drawn from various home-service battalions of the Regiment, and Frank was chosen because despite his young age – he was now 19 – he was a full corporal. Taken by train to Folkestone, Frank crossed by transport ship to Boulogne on 26 July 1916. Posted to a holding unit at an Infantry Base Depot nearby, he was sent with the draft to join the 11th Battalion at Henencourt Wood on the Somme on 29 July; the battalion War Diary records that 13 officers and 530 men joined that day, giving an indication of just how many casualties there had been a few weeks before. There was little time to acclimatise, and within a day Frank found himself heading up to the trenches on the Somme front. The battalion took over positions near the village of Bazentin le Petit, opposite Intermediate Trench. This rather strange position ran parallel to a small track coming out of the village towards a wood known as High Wood; a place already with a deadly reputation and the scene of several failed attacks. In front of Intermediate Trench Frank and the 11th Suffolks not only had the Germans ahead of them, but also across to their right in High Wood, and to their far left in the village of Poziéres. He later recalled:

> When I arrived in France we went to Boulogne and from there to Etaples for a fortnight to the Bull Ring. It was a devil! I was lucky; I had boil come on my chin and I went sick the first day. The doctor said sit down in my chair, he'd only got a little shed with a table and one chair, and he got my chin over his arm, picked up a knife cut the damn off and chucked it out sideways without putting anything on. I was put on light duties and had to report every day, and at the end of the first week he did the same. So as a consequence I never went to the Bull Ring. I was at the Somme, but only just got there and after a week was away.[3]

Thankfully this was only a short tour of duty in the line, and just over a week later the battalion was marching out of the Somme towards a railhead at Mericourt. From here the slow trains, with their box cars packed with soldiers, took them to Northern France for a change of sector. Here they took over trenches close to the village of Bois-Grenier, just south of the town of Armentières. The line here had not moved for nearly two years and it was considered a 'quiet' sector. Quiet sectors were a bit of a misnomer in the Great War, as they were always places of activity on both sides, and the daily casualties reflected that. But as August moved into September on the Armentières front, Frank's battalion and the division they were a part of, the 34th Division, began to prepare for the coming autumn and winter. Although Frank had not been with them at that time, the division had previously served in this area before the Somme, and in the cold days of early 1916. They knew that aside from enemy shell fire, one of the greatest problems here was the elements; a fairly flat landscape with severe drainage problems, trenches were prone to flooding, and that combined with heavy snow and cold made life on the front line very hard. This time they were determined to be prepared and one of the Staff Officers of the 34th Division later wrote:

> we were settling down for the winter, so I had to make sure that every man went into the line in dry gum boots, and came out to dry service boots and puttees. As to socks, I had to see that every man in the line got a dry clean pair every morning. That was easy as we had the big laundry at Armentières in those days . . . We had also rest-houses in the support line, one to each battalion front. These were in the cellars of ruined houses, and necessarily very close to the front line. In the rest house a man who had collapsed from cold after being some hours in a listening post, where no movement was possible, or one who had fallen into a shell hole and got wet through, or a man simply knocked out by fatigue, could be brought. He was stripped, put into dry blankets before a fire, given soup and cocoa while his clothes dried, and sent on his way generally fit again after a few hours.[4]

The winter of 1916/17 proved to be the harshest of the war, with temperatures in Northern France dropping to at least − 20°. Because of these arrangements, not commonplace in most divisions on the British front, casualties from the elements were minimised and Frank, like the majority of men in his platoon, survived without any sickness. Frank also now found himself promoted to sergeant, second in command of his platoon, with a young officer, a second lieutenant, being the platoon commander. At full strength there were less than fifty men in a platoon, and at this time the Army did things in fours: it marched in fours, there were

British troops move to take part in the Battle of Arras, April 1917.

four infantry sections in a platoon, four platoons in an infantry company and four companies in a battalion – in this case 11th Battalion Suffolk Regiment. With promotion came a change of sector, to Arras, where Frank would remain for the next few months. The arrangements for the troops in the front line were not as good as at Armentières and the cold weather continued into March 1917 with heavy snow, and sub-zero temperatures. Frank was admitted to a Field Ambulance with 'P.U.O.' as it states in his medical papers. This translates as Pyrexia of Unknown or Undetermined Origin; basically a temperature caused by an unknown condition or infection. A common cause at this time of year was a cold or virus caused by the weather, but body lice, which every soldier was infected with, and which lived in and laid eggs in the seams of their Service Dress tunic and trousers, could also be a cause. Lice, picked up in the farm buildings used as billets, and spread through close contact with a soldier's comrades, were the bane of soldiers lives and could cause 'trench fever'. Trench fever was a debilitating illness with a high fever, with headache, limb pain and a rash also common. Normally it lasted around five days, but extreme cases could see men hospitalised and even returned to Britain for treatment. It would appear Frank was struck down with this as he was sent from a Field Ambulance on the battlefield to a Casualty Clearing Station west of Arras, and from here to 11th General Hospital at Camiers, on the French coast near

Boulogne. Hospitalised here until mid-April, Frank recovered and was back with his battalion in late April, now heavily involved in the Battle of Arras.

The fighting at Arras in April and May 1917 would become one of Britain's most costly battles in the Great War. From the 9 April until the battle ended in mid-May on average there were more than 4,000 casualties each day with a total of 159,000 casualties by the end of the battle, and one of those would be Frank Plumb. The 11th Suffolks had been in action since the first attack on 9 April, and when Frank rejoined them on the 20th they were in rest at Monts en Ternois, a small village some miles west of Arras, where they had just been paraded and inspected by the divisional commander, Major General Nicholson. Frank had missed that, and when he got back to his platoon found a lot of friends gone and new faces in their place, due to the recent casualties at Arras. A few days later they marched to a hutted camp near Arras, and from here went into the trenches opposite the village of Roeux on the night of 24/25 April. This area had been captured at the beginning of the battle but progress had since been slow. The village was dominated by a large agricultural chemical factory, and was riddled with tunnels. The strong positions and the Germans clever use of the tunnels had meant that so far the British had little to show but casualties for all the fighting. On 27 April Frank's commanding officer was called to Brigade Headquarters close to Arras and was given the orders that would take the battalion into the next attack at Roeux. Zero Hour was 4.27 am on the 28th, when Frank and his men went in.

We were to attack a village where there had been a huge chemical works and we were Over The Top there on April 28th. I was in charge of my platoon as I'd lost my officer; I was platoon sergeant. We started off. My platoon laid out in the snow until our people put a barrage on the German front lines and then mine and another platoon were behind the first wave, and our orders were as soon as the barrage lifts to advance. We crossed No Man's Land and I had to jump into this eight foot [deep] front line trench and I could see our first wave going along and they were dropping down in sections, so I got on the fire step to get up and there is all barbed wire above, and I looked for a way to get out and as I stooped down a grenade burst right in front of my head and I got my tin hat on, and got covered with pieces. I got pieces in my head, my hand, my wrists. But if I hadn't looked down I would have got it right in my face. Of course that blew me off the fire step and I landed on my head and shoulders. Just then one of the headquarters officers came down and said 'good gracious sergeant, are you hurt?' He helped me up, and . . . there was blood on my hands, and he saw a patch coming out of my stripes, and he said 'Get back to the dressing station'. And that was me out and . . . I went about 200 yards and I was into a meadow which was much lower than the ground I had come out of, and there was a river, the Scarpe. I went through this meadow and a railway embankment crossed over so there was a bridge. Here barges used to go up and down, and on one side was a wide path for horses to drag these barges. Well our dressing station was there, dug into the embankment. In that meadow was a man calling out 'Walking Cases Here'. He said don't try to get here, as they were shelling. Go across there to another dressing station. There was a floating bridge on the water, only like duckboards, and then there was a tight wire over the top, and we held it and got across with four or five men behind me, and very soon I was up to my knees in water. Getting on further I was going past some trees when a man popped out and said 'Sergeant come over here!' He was a Sergeant and there was a gun under those trees, partly camouflaged. He said 'I've just made a cup of tea, come in!' I was a little way in front of the other men, so I went in and he gave me a good dose of rum in a hot cup of tea. I had six kilometres then to walk, back to Arras and this other dressing station. They then loaded me up in an ambulance. One man had an arm wound, and the roads were terrible, and this thing only had solid tires; he was screaming all the time. I held on to the door for what it was worth and when we got to hospital they dug pieces [of the grenade] out of my wrists . . . and then they found a hole, and put a probe in and turned and turned, and the Doctor said 'I can feel it, I can feel it!' . . . he carefully drew it out and he laid it along a rule; two and half inches![5]

The attack had taken place south-west of the village of Roeux. Frank's battalion had advanced from support positions close to the Scarpe Valley with a wooded area called Mount Pleasant Wood on their right, taken by the 10th Lincolns, and a position called Ceylon Trench ahead of them on the edge of Roeux village. This is where Frank had been wounded, and he was one of a number of men the battalion lost at this time. Their War Diary records that 17 officers and 610 men had gone into battle, and 7 officers and 325 men made it back.[6] Despite these casualties, once again the chemical works and much of the village remained in German hands, and it would only be at the end of the battle that the area was finally cleared.

Frank, with his shrapnel wounds from the German grenade, ended up at the 7th Canadian General Hospital at Etaples. He remained here for a few weeks until his treatment was at an end and was then posted to an Infantry Base Depot, also located at Etaples. Frank was disappointed his wound wasn't a 'Blighty One' – a wound serious enough to take a soldier back home to Blighty; the word soldiers used for Britain during the Great War, derived from an Indian word for 'home' used by old soldiers in India before the war. And to add insult to injury, while he had previously escaped the Bull Ring, the main training area for the Army located at Etaples with its feared and hated instructors called 'Canaries' due to their yellow armbands, this time he found himself here for two weeks in intensive physical drill and battle training. It was late May when he finally got back to his platoon, where he found them and the battalion at rest in the village of Pernois on the Somme, close to the city of Amiens. But he barely had time to enjoy this rest before the battalion was on the move again, this time to a new sector.

> I was called to headquarters and first thing they introduced a young officer who had just come out. They told me that he had no practical experience and he's the son of a wealthy father and just got his commission . . . The second thing they told me was that the French had called on us for some help at St Quentin . . . they asked if we could do a fresh do close by to draw German troops away from St Quentin. Our division was one selected and we went on the march, and to Peronne. Just before we got to the town of Peronne, that was a town where there were several main roads that ran through it, we could see some men on horseback coming across country. We were halted and they came up to us, and they were Australians, Australian Light Horse. It was them we were going to relieve [at Hargicourt]. They dismounted . . . and one man guided us round Peronne. He said we were lucky to be here as they had been there a month and had no trouble. We were on the ridge of a big valley, and they weren't continuous trenches, they were strong points. The Australian said 'You'll have a cushy time here!' I said to my men I wouldn't mind betting we'll be going over the top in a few days, and I was right![7]

Frank was right. On 26 August 1917 his battalion took part in an attack on the Hindenburg Line positions held by the Germans north-east of the village of Hargicourt. The objective was Triangle Trench, a German-held line close to Quennemont Farm on the rising ground beyond. A minor operation, it involved several battalions of the 34th Division and the 11th Suffolks' War Diary recalled:

> It was a very cold night and therefore the men were very cold before starting off . . . The battalion went over in two waves . . . At the junction of Sugar and Malakoff Trench there was hand to hand fighting and bombing, the Machine Guns here caused a few casualties but the crew was soon killed . . . On reaching the objective on the right O.C. [Officer Commanding] D Company noticed Triangle Trench was strongly occupied and he immediately decided to push on and take it, this he did and got thirty prisoners.[8]

Among the men who cleared Triangle Trench that day was Corporal Sidney James Day. Day had originally served with the 9th Suffolks on the Somme, and after being wounded joined the 11th. A battalion bomber, his team of men armed with Mills hand grenades fought their way into the trench and captured it. At one point a German grenade landed among a group of men, including two officers, and he immediately picked it up and threw it over the trench, saving the lives of those present. For his bravery at Hargicourt he was subsequently awarded a Victoria Cross.[9] Although Frank did not know Day personally, he was always proud to be associated with a battalion that a member of which had been awarded the highest medal for bravery.

Men of the 11th Battalion Suffolk Regiment, France 1918.

A quiet period in the Hargicourt sector followed with tours in and out of the trenches into early October 1917. Then the 11th Suffolks moved north into Belgium to take part in the Third Battle of Ypres, better known as Passchendaele. They would suffer heavy casualties in the mud and mire of Flanders, but Frank was spared that experience; just as his battalion was about to move up he was admitted to a Field Ambulance with scabies and was hospitalised. By the time he was discharged in November, the battle was over and he was due some home leave, and got a few days back at Copdock before he rejoined the unit. By the time he returned they were holding positions south of Arras, close to the village of Croisilles. Here they would remain for the winter of 1917/18.

By February 1918 the war was taking a new turn. America had entered the conflict the previous spring, and it was now a matter of months or weeks before large numbers of their troops took to the field and tipped the balance in the favour of the allies. Aware of this, the German High Command realised that the only way potentially to end the war in Germany's favour was to end the war on two fronts; despite the Russian Revolution in 1917 they were still taking part in operations on the Eastern Front. Therefore, in February the Treaty of Brest-Litovsk was signed, ending the war in the East and realising thousands of German troops for fighting in the West. With preparations for this last 'roll of the dice' complete, the first stage was launched between the Somme and the positions south of Arras on 21 March 1918, in an operation the Germans called the *Kaiserschlact* – the Kaiser's Battle. Frank's battalion found themselves in the thick of it near Croisilles and the nearby village of Fontaine.

> On the 21st March 1918 a runner came along to tell us to Stand To! I'd had six weeks where I hadn't had my shoes off and I thought I'd get a clean pair of socks, and I'll change them. I sat down on the fire step near the sentry and had just started to undo one of my puttees, shells started dropping everywhere, and this was in broad daylight – the sun was shining! I jumped up on the fire step and looked over, and do you know right across the German lines, I could see for miles, there was rows and rows of Germans, single file – rows about a hundred yards apart. Here and there was a horse drawn vehicle and I could see about two of what were the first German tanks. They didn't seem to be coming straight for me, I was right on the extreme left as we faced the Germans, they seemed to be coming across at an angle in front of me. Well I had got three other sections who could see further round, and I left one section in two bits of trench with a

buttress so they wouldn't get killed, and went further on to look. Well, we held them that day and I went again the next day and when I came back . . . a shell dropped in my section, and blew me over backwards and crashed me on my back. I went forwards as soon as I could and as soon as I got round the buttress there was a man's leg, where a man's body had been there was a hole, his head was just the other side, one was laid flat on his back, and as I looked at him he raised himself up to a sitting position. He was a man who had been with me quite a long time . . . his eyes opened, but absolutely blank. Then they cleared he looked straight at me, and said 'Plummie!' – well I know that was what they called me among themselves but I had never had one call me that; it has always been Sergeant before. As he said that he looked down, and my eyes followed his. All his stomach and blood was coming through his trousers and he suddenly flopped back. Just then two stretcher bearers came tearing down . . . they dropped the stretcher down, grabbed him and away they went with him. The rest . . . were all dead.

Then a runner came tearing down the trench . . . who said you've got to get your platoon and come back to headquarters as quickly as possible, the Germans have broken through . . . and they are trying to get round behind us . . . I got back to headquarters and there was just an officer waiting . . . who said we had to catch the others up and get back a few miles quickly or we would be surrounded. I could hear rifles and machine guns going off back behind us. So we were going like mad, and we got into a sunken road and called a stop. Well I dropped on the bank as soon as we stopped and I was asleep in a moment. The next thing there was an officer kicking and punching me to wake up. He said we had to get away before daylight . . . and away we went. We got through and we were fighting and going back until the 30th April. By that time we were practically asleep standing up.[10]

Frank later confessed that while he could remember the beginning and the end of the fighting that spring, first at Arras in March and then in Flanders as part of what became the Battle of the Lys in April 1918, much of it was a blur. He felt as if he had been running around like a headless chicken, and in some ways that mirrored the fortunes of the British Army. The Germans had broken through in March, but eventually stopped just short of Amiens and along the River Ancre near Albert. In April they had retaken all the ground around Ypres fought over in 1917, and to the south in France

'Backs to the Wall': British troops defending during the Battle of Lys, April 1918.

overrun ground that had not seen a shot fired since the start of the war in 1914. But both offensives had run out of steam, with heavy losses on both sides – losses that for Germany were almost irreplaceable by this stage in the war as their conscription increasingly failed to cope with replacing those killed and wounded, and their industry was on its knees, crippled by allied blockades.

For Frank and the 11th Suffolks, by late April it was clear in Flanders that the situation had reached stalemate again. The German attacks had come to an and, and while the line saw the nearby city of Ypres sitting in even more of a vulnerable position than it had previously occupied, with the Germans in positions to the south-west of it as well as in front, no breakthrough had been made. The last few days of the month were spent in a camp on rest, and digging reserve trenches close to the hamlet of Brandhoek. It was here, in one of the old camps now very close to the front line, that Frank's war came to an end on 30 April. The War Diary records 'several casualties' during this period. After all that heavy fighting, Frank was wounded in a quiet period.

At the camp I was given a hut for the men and we were told get what sleep you can: there's no guard duty tonight. I just dropped down with the others and our transport came along and I had to look after them; they brought ammunition, rations and other kit. Just then there was a yell for platoon commanders at headquarters at once, so I had to tear off. There was the Colonel outside, who said 'Sorry to call you out gentleman, but I've just had some bad news. You see that big hill over there, that's Kemmel Hill and I've just had word to say the Germans have captured the top of the hill'. It was beginning to turn dark and just as he said that we could see German Very Lights going up this side of the top. He then said we would have to be out of there by daylight, as soon as daylight came up we would be in full view. So I went back to the hut and one of my corporal's home was in the next village to mine in Suffolk. He said there was a parcel for me. I looked and there was a tin with a cake that my mother had made and she had sent me for my birthday; this was the 30th April and my birthday was the 5th May. It was done up in canvas, and I sat on the floor with it, and I remember leaning back to get my knife to cut the stitches and the next thing I knew was a woman's voice saying 'Oh Sergeant, you are waking up at last!'[11]

A large calibre shell had landed on the road outside, and a huge fragment had come through the wall of the hut and hit Frank in the cheek, lifting him several feet into the air. It smashed all his teeth and his jaw was hanging by sinews. It also ruptured his spine, and as he was loaded on a stretcher and then put in an ambulance, every movement was agony. The battalion Medical Officer, he later found out, thought that he wouldn't survive. But having woken up in 83rd General Hospital at Boulogne, it was the start of his recovery but his face was a complete mess. Facial injuries in the war were all too commonplace. The power of bullets and shell fragments to smash and disfigure a man's face became all too apparent as the war progressed. Facial reconstruction, what is now known as plastic surgery, was very much in its infancy, but did exist. The Gillies Archive at Queen Mary's Hopsital, Sidcup, is the only surviving collection of papers of men who were these early 'guinea pigs'. Frank was never admitted here, but when he got back to England, he later recalled that he was lucky to be sent to a hospital where an American surgeon worked who had specialised in facial injuries. This man rebuilt Frank's lower jaw and brought in Army dentists to remove the damaged teeth and eventually fit him with dentures. At one stage his whole jaw was wired up, and skin from other parts of the

A huge shell blast; Frank Plumb was wounded by such a blast in April 1918.

body had been used to repair the damaged lower face. Even six months later he couldn't eat solid food, but by November he was deemed fit for discharge, and ten days after the Armistice was signed he was officially discharged from the Army, 'no longer physically fit to serve', and issued with a rail warrant. No one spoke to him on the journey home as his face still looked such a mess, but his mother was waiting at Ipswich station where she greeted him with open arms and relieved him of the huge Army kitbag he was carrying, which in his weakened state he was struggling to cope with.

Like many men, Frank's war was now officially over but he was only just starting to come to terms with the consequences of it. His medical papers show that it would still be several months before he could eat solids, his jaw despite the reconstruction would never be as strong as it once was, and for the rest of his life he could really only eat small meals. He stayed in Suffolk until his retirement when he moved to Sussex, and following the death of his wife moved into a disabled ex-serviceman's home called Gifford House in Worthing. At the age of 92 he was a tall, sprightly man, but the faint traces of his facial wounds were still visible. Frank's injury had not been as severe as many of those chronicled in the Gillies Archive, but they and Frank were the early guinea pigs of reconstructive surgery, which would be

Frank Plumb in his later years at Gifford House, Worthing.

so prominent a generation later in the Second World War when men like Frank would be called on again to serve their country and suffer crippling injuries, always noted under the generic and comforting word 'casualties'.

Researching Frank Plumb

A starting point for research into men like Frank Plumb who were grievously wounded in the war are the so-called 'Pension Records' in class WO364 at TNA. These records are somewhat poorly named as they are not in fact pension records; they are the service records of men discharged from the Army and awarded a pension, or men discharged who were potentially entitled to one, but never received it. These records were stored separately from the main service records, so badly affected by bombing in the Second World War, and used by the Ministry of Pensions and latterly by the Department of Social Security. Frank's record was kept in this class because of his on-going treatment following the war, and the fact that his final years were spent in a government-sponsored care home in Worthing. Sometimes these records, which can be seen on microfilm at TNA or online at Ancestry, contain only brief information on military service and are heavy on documents relating to the medical treatment of the soldier. The reasons for this is that these records were largely kept to prove or disprove entitlement to pension, so as long as one document proved when a man served, they were not too concerned about the finer detail. The exception to this are claims relating to battle wounds or injury. In this case the so-called 'Casualty Form – Active Service' is nearly always retained because this shows all of the overseas medical treatment of men while on active service abroad. This includes the date a man was wounded, the type of wound and what medical facilities he was admitted to. The most common type of wound noted is 'GSW', which is indeed noted on Frank's sheet for the Arras period. This was a Gun Shot Wound, and while it normally relates to receiving a bullet wound from a rifle or machine gun, it was also used to classify injuries from shrapnel balls. These were small lead or steel balls, a little smaller than a musket ball, that were contained inside shrapnel shells which burst in the air, raining down hundreds of such balls per shell. Common medical facilities mentioned in these documents are 'FA' and 'CCS' – Field Ambulances and Casualty Clearing Stations respectively. The Field Ambulance was a unit run by Royal Army Medical Corps and based close to the front. Wounded soldiers would be stabilised here, assessed and then loaded onto ambulances and taken to the Casualty Clearing Station, which was generally several miles from the front. Covering a square mile of ground, this contained operating theatres, X-ray wards, blood-transfusion units and was staffed by Army nurses as well as medical personnel. Lists of both Field Ambulances and Casualty Clearing Stations can be found on the Long, Long Trail website, in some cases showing their exact location. Each FA and CCS also has a War Diary which is in class WO95 at TNA.

Frank Plumb's movements were followed using the 11th Battalion Suffolk Regiment's War Diary and luckily Frank had agreed to be interviewed about his war in the 1990s. While this interview is in the author's private collection, there are several public archives most notably at the Imperial War Museum in London. It is always worth contacting such an archive to see if your relative was interviewed or submitted a written account.

Although there is no mention of Frank Plumb in the Gillies Archive, their website contains fascinating images and information on those with facial wounds, and they have also listed all the men contained in the files that survive. They are gradually researching each of these men and welcome contact from families with further information.

Notes

1. T.J. Mitchell, *Medical Services: Casualties and Medical Statistics of the Great War* (1931), p. 14.
2. Interview with author, 1988.
3. Ibid.
4. J. Shakespear, *The Thirty Fourth Division 1915–1919* (H.F. & G. Witherby, 1921), pp. 77–8.
5. Interview with author, 1988.
6. 11th Battalion Suffolk Regiment War Diary TNA WO95/2458. Crown Copyright.
7. Interview with author, 1988.
8. 11th Battalion Suffolk Regiment War Diary TNA WO95/2458.
9. Sidney James Day survived the war and died in Hampshire in 1959.
10. Interview with author, 1988.
11. Ibid.

Chapter Ten

FROM OFFICER TO PRIVATE

The Strange Case of Ernest Hopcraft

Ernest George de Lathom Hopcraft was arguably the epitome of an Edwardian gentleman. A man of money, he had been born in Rugby in 1886, the son of a brewer and Justice of the Peace, who owned and ran the Hopcraft Brewey in Brackley, Northamptonshire. He grew up on the huge estate of Walton Hall, near Milton Keynes, which today is the headquarters of the Open University, and later also lived near Banbury. Educated at Harrow public school, by the 1910s he described himself as a 'gentleman'. Within a few years he would join the Army as an officer, be court-martialled and dismissed, re-enlist as a private soldier and die on the battlefield in the last months of the war. What had gone so badly wrong to bring about such a tragic conclusion to an otherwise seemingly promising life?

Ernest Hopcraft's first attempt to join the military came in May 1911. After Harrow he had gone on to Jesus College, Cambridge, and had graduated with a Batchelor's degree in 1909. He had been a member of the Officer Training Corps both at school and university, and it was not uncommon for the sons of men with money, like Ernest, to go into the Army if no other trade apparently interested them. However, the strict medical examination that all potential officers had to undertake exposed some medical problems – varicose veins and poor eyesight – which excluded him joining as an officer of the regular Army. With not inconsiderable personal means, he instead moved to Brighton and lived the life of a gentleman there until the outbreak of war in 1914. He later

Ernest Hopcraft as an officer of the 13th Battalion Middlesex Regiment, 1916.

stated: 'I did not think it of any use to join at the out-break of war, but early in 1915 I made up my mind to do so. I was then rejected four times on account of the varicose veins by the doctors of the Inns of Court OTC, London University OTC, Artist's Rifles and Royal Naval Division.[1] All of these were quite common routes into the Army as an officer for a man of his background. The Inns of Court Officer Training Corps and that of London University enlisted thousands of men in the early phase of the war who were later commissioned, and by 1915 the Artist's Rifles had essentially become a funnel for suitable men seeking to become officers. The Royal Naval Division, Britain's sea soldiers, were also actively recruiting at Crystal Palace, and again many ended up serving as ratings in the division before become an officer. Despite all these false starts eventually Ernest did obtain a commission as a second lieutenant in the Middlesex Regiment: 'I had a recommendation for a commission and was finally passed by a local doctor at Brighton, being gazetted on May 15th 1915 to the 13th Middlesex . . . at Shoreham on sea'.[2]

Following officer training he was posted to the reserve battalion at Shoreham, where the British Army had established a large training camp overlooking the sea. On the high ground here, the battalion marched and trained, and Hopcraft began life as an infantry platoon commander. Following the tremendous losses on the Western Front in 1915, replacements, especially among officers, were needed in France by the Middlesex Regiment. This large regiment had numerous battalions on active service, and by this stage of the conflict the life expectancy of platoon commanders like Ernest could be measured in weeks, and a constant stream of them were required overseas. He therefore crossed to France, travelling from Folkestone to Boulogne, on 17 April 1916. After a few days at the base, he was sent to the 11th Battalion Middlesex Regiment, a battalion in the 12th (Eastern) Division. This unit had been in France for nearly a year and had taken some losses at the Battle of Loos in September and October 1915. At the time Ernest joined them they were still in the Loos sector, holding the trenches close to the Hulluch Quarries. The previous month had seen bitter fighting in this area, with the 11th Middlesex heavily involved, but now it was considered 'quiet'. On 27 April this was to prove a false hope when the Germans launched a major gas attack in the Hulluch sector. Ernest and his battalion were not in the line at the time, as the whole division had just been relieved; Scottish and Irish troops were the ones directly affected but the size and scope of the gas used meant that it drifted, and in some cases was fired, into billets behind the lines. The battalion War Diary records that they were affected by it in the village of Sailly Labourse, some miles from the trenches. A witness from a neighbouring battalion later recalled:

> at 7 o'clock the dread sound of Strombos horns from the direction of Vermelles warned us of an impending gas attack. A few moments later we saw a blue cloud approaching from far away . . . [we] stood-to and all ranks put on their smoke helmets without an instants delay. The helmets in use at this time consisted of grey flannel bags soaked in chemicals and fitted with a talc window; they had a somewhat suffocating effect . . . We had scarcely got into our helmets when the gas cloud, as thick as a London fog, gradually enveloped us, making it impossible to see more than a few yards.[3]

Although it was a discomforting experience, there had been no casualties and for now Ernest's brief experience of front-line service was over. As the battalion had been in the trenches for some time since the Battle of Loos, it was due for a period of rest behind the lines. They therefore marched to the village of Marles les Mines, located some miles south-west of the town of Bethune. Untouched by war, and still full of civilians, the battalion spent the next six weeks here and when it did march back to the battlefield area it was put in reserve and only required to supply men for working parties.

Unbeknown to Ernest and the men in his battalion, plans for the Battle of the Somme were about to be put into place and their division was needed as reserve troops to be ready as and when the breakthrough on the Somme was made. By late June they were in camp near the town of Albert and on the first day of the battle, 1 July 1916, things had not gone to plan; there was no breakthrough, only heavy losses. The 11th Middlesex therefore was called up some days later to take over trenches in front of Mash Valley at Ovillers. This ground had seen a disastrous attack on the first day, and on 7 July Ernest and the men of his platoon went over the top in the next phase of the fighting. Units of their division had already captured trenches on the edge of the village of Ovillers and the Middlesex were sent to re-enforce the position. The somewhat confused fighting, with no clear front line, and men from several units scattered around a small area, was an odd introduction to battle for Ernest, and it was likely with some relief that they left the battlefield at Mash Valley and returned to billets. However, their involvement with the Somme was far from over and throughout the rest of the month and on into September they were in and out of the trenches at Ovillers and Poziéres. By this time conditions on the Somme were very poor. 'One of the main difficulties the troops had to contend with . . . was the mud, which was very deep and sticky, in many places men being unable to move without assistance'.[4]

In October 1916 the battalion took over positions between the villages of Flers and Guedecourt. A few weeks before tanks had been used here for the first time, and Ernest and his platoon had marched past the wrecks of some on the way to the line. The ground here was rising and gave good views towards the town of Bapaume, the main German railhead in this sector, and which had been an objective on the first day of the battle. One witness serving with the 12th (Eastern) Division described the battlefield at this time:

> The sector occupied by the 36th Brigade [of which 11th Middlesex was a part] was not an easy one. The front line, Grid Support and Grid Trench, consisted of old German trenches, and the support line was some 500 yards in the rear. The communication trench between Grid Support and Grid Trench was only two feet deep and in full view of the enemy. The main approach to the trenches from the rear was down an open valley, into which shells dropped almost unceasingly.[5]

An attack to push the lines even further forward here was planned for 7 October, and the 11th Middlesex would be in reserve, ready to move forward and take over any captured positions from the assault troops of the Royal Fusiliers. Ernest Hopcraft's role in this was to act as the eyes of his company commander, and reconnoitre the ground the men were to move in. His actions here were something he was later proud of and wrote: 'Captain Peploe . . . was well satisfied with my work, especially at Guedecourt in October 1916 when I did very well in reconnaissance'.[6]

At the end of the month the battalion left the Somme and moved to the area around the city of Arras in Northern France, prior to moving into the Arras trenches proper. Arras was now an important part of the British line on the Western Front, and many units were being rotated through going to and from the Somme. By November they experienced their first tour of the front line here, and as the weather got progressively colder they began to settle down to periods in the trenches and rest in billets beyond Arras.

It was at about this time that Ernest Hopcraft volunteered to take up duties as a town major. Town majors were British officers put in charge of major locations like Arras, or smaller villages regularly used as billeting areas by the Army. Their job was to manage and police the village, establish relations with the local French civilian population, pay them for the use of ground and buildings required as billets and compensate them for any losses caused by theft or wilful damage. Few records of town majors survive, but those that do offer a fascinating insight into local negotiations, which could be tricky at the best of times. The British Army rarely disputed claims of loss, and as this became widely known such claims were more and more commonplace. No doubt some town majors felt the odd French person was exploiting the situation, and occasionally relations could be strained because of this. On the other hand, the local population in Northern France had little say in the mass invasion of British troops, with different ideas and values, and perhaps not as considerate of other people's property in wartime as they might have been before 1914. For Ernest an incident with the locals would sadly define his time as an officer. He later recalled the episode in a letter to the War Office:

> I had previously done three weeks as Town Major at Gouy-en-Artois, near Arras, in November 1916, when the Town Major of that village was on leave, and was chosen as Town Major for Houvin-Houvigneul near Frévent where I arrived on December 24th 1916. There I had much difficulty in finding officers billets as the villagers were not at all willing to give the rooms. I was told by the mayor that officer's billets were to be had at a certain house occupied by Mlle Rouget. I was also asked by some officers to see about a bedroom in that house which was constantly kept locked up and disused on the pretext that a French soldier was returning from leave very shortly. I went with the officers to this house and found a soldier there on this occasion, but was repeatedly and violently ordered out by Mlle Rouget when I enquired about the room. I left as I was told by the soldier that he was using the room, though I did not believe it as I had overheard Mlle Rouget tell the soldier to say this. Therefore when another officer, Lieutenant Sanderson 69th Field Company RE, came for a billet shortly afterwards I showed him this house as there was a large sitting room vacant and I hoped to find out more about the bedroom in question . . . On account of my previous reception I did not speak to Mlle Rouget when I went in. However she came up and furiously ordered us out many times. I took no notice and talked to Lieutenant Sanderson. This made her worse and she tried to push Lt Sanderson out and slapped him on the head. On this I lost my temper and gave her a box on the ear, with the open hand, not a hard blow with the fist. However she fell down and screamed, as I thought from temper. A girl then came in and remonstrated. I told her simply

Men of the 2/20th Battalion London Regiment.

what had happened. I then left as I did not think that Mlle Rouget was screaming because she was really hurt. Nothing more occurred.[7]

Unfortunately for Ernest the matter did not end there. Mademoiselle Rouget reported the matter to the local mayor, who reported it to a senior British officer. Ernest was immediately arrested by the Military Police and charged with 'committing an offence against the person of a resident'.[8] The records of the court martial that followed do not survive, but it seems that Rouget was well connected and given Ernest's position of responsibility, and the fact that he had struck a woman, the court found against him and he was subsequently found guilty and officially dismissed from the Army in February 1917. By the 22nd he was back in Folkestone, and went home to his property in Brighton. He was outraged at having been treated in such a way, and wrote to the War Office to try and get his case heard again and have his commission reinstated: 'I most profoundly regret the incident which was done in a moment of hasty temper, and I admit I should not have done so. I humbly beg you to reconsider the case in my favour and reinstate my position'.[9] However, there was little chance that the War Office would look at such an appeal favourably. It was rare for the verdict of a court martial to be overturned, and most likely the military authorities worried how such a move might affect relations with the French population. That relationship was worth more than the career and reputation of one officer, and so the outcome and response was almost guaranteed.

> With reference to your undated latter, I am commanded to inform you that the Army Council have carefully considered the appeal therein embodied in conjunction with the proceedings of the General Court Martial by which you were recently convicted, but they regret that they can discover no ground for interfering with the finding or sentence of the Court.[10]

It would have been easy at this point for Ernest Hopcraft to slip into obscurity. Having been dishonourably discharged he was not eligible for further military service as a conscript. He could have walked away from the Army, and as a man of means with money one day to inherit from his father, he could have lived comfortably for the rest of his life. But Ernest chose not to do this. His actions in the French village had been wrong, he knew that. But he was determined to prove himself worthy again and in his mind the only thing to do was to re-enlist. But enlistment as an officer again was impossible. The only route open to him was to join as an ordinary soldier.

A month or so later, in the early spring of 1917, he went to London and joined the Rifle Brigade as a rifleman. It is likely he chose London as people in Brighton might ask questions if he attempted to enlist there and he had no past history in London, and it was big enough to be anonymous in. Now as an ordinary soldier he began training all over again; how a man used to

A contemporary illustration of the 2/20th Londons in Palestine, 1917.

Moving up to the attack at Flesquieres in September 1918, from the regimental history.

command, and the language of command, fared under such conditions can only be imagined, and one wonders how he didn't give himself and his previous service away. But there is no trace of any reason for the Army to connect him with previous events and discharge him again, as they likely would have done, and speaks volume for the sort of man that he was, that he stuck at it, seemingly without complaint. Now at Winchester with his regiment he was soon after posted to the 3/20th Battalion London Regiment (Blackheath and Woolwich), a reserve unit based in Essex. Once training was complete by the summer of 1917, he was sent overseas to join an active battalion of the regiment, in this case the 2/20th Battalion, then serving in Palestine with the 60th (London) Division. He joined them in the desert on a battlefield in great contrast to the muddy trenches of the Somme he had experienced the year before. He fought with the battalion in the capture of Jerusalem in December 1917, and moved with them from Palestine to France in the summer of 1918 when British units in Palestine were gradually being substituted for Indian army ones, so that fresh battalions could be sent to the Western Front.

Back in France he took part in operations on the Hindenburg Line in August and September of 1918, as his battalion advanced on the villages of Havrincourt and then towards Flesquieres. On 27 September the battalion made an attack towards the deep trenches of the Hindenburg Line west of Flesquieres village. The battalion history records:

> the Brown Line was captured with a rush, and companies pushed on some distance down Scull Trench and along the ridge running east of Flesquieres to Premy Support Trench where it was necessary to halt . . . The advance of the battalion had been uniformly successful, and 520 prisoners, 6 field guns, 34 machine guns, and 6 trench mortars had been captured . . . [on] their final objective – the Blue Line – they became heavily engaged . . . One section came across a party of the enemy with machine guns. The enemy raised their hands in token that they surrendered, and when Lieutenant Slaughter and his men advanced towards them to take them prisoners, they opened fire with a machine gun. As a result Lieut Slaughter was killed, and there were several other casualties.[11]

No first-hand account of exactly what happened next survives but the one hint at the events that unfolded on that French hillside is contained in the text of a memorial to Ernest Hopcraft which hangs on the wall of a Northamptonshire church: 'He fell in action, at the assault on the German Hindenburg Line at Marcoing near Cambrai September 27th 1918; 5 weeks and 4 days before the Armistice. Gone but never forgotten. At the battle of Flesquieres near Marcoing he gallantly attacked, single handed a German machine gun post and was killed.'[12] With the death of his platoon commander, and a critical situation developing, did Ernest Hopcraft's previous training as an officer kick in? Did he see himself perhaps in a position to redeem himself? We shall never know as the burst of fire

The plaque to Ernest Hopcraft in the church at Middleton Chenery. (Photograph: Andy Lonergan)

brought his war, his chance of redemption in the eyes of the War Office and his life to an end.

After the war his father, like many thousands of others, sought to memorialise his son. He placed a memorial in the church the family had connections with in Middleton Cheney near Banbury. From his other home in Brighton he applied for Ernest's medals but according to the medal records, they were initially refused as Ernest had forfeited his entitlement to medals as an officer due to the court martial. However, his second period of service did entitle him to the British War and Victory medals and these were despatched to his father along with a bronze Memorial Plaque and paper Memorial Scroll in the 1920s. All of these medals were named to the ordinary soldier Ernest had died as, with no reference to his status as an officer. At about the same time his old school, Harrow, was in the

Ernest Hopcraft's unusual grave at Flesquieres Hill Cemetery.

process of compiling the information to produce a printed roll of honour with photographs and contacted Hopcraft senior. Understandably he was keen to downplay the events of Ernest's early service, but at the same time not wanting to admit his son had died as a private, and so submitted a photograph of Ernest in officer's uniform. While the Harrow roll mentioned Ernest Hopcraft's death with the 2/20th London Regiment, it gave the clear impression he was still a junior officer, as befitting his class and background – or at least it glossed over what his rank actually was at the time of death. Sometime later the father was contacted again, this time by the Imperial War Graves Commission. At this point they were in the process of making the war cemeteries on the Western Front permanent. Ernest had originally been buried on the battlefield close to where he fell, but in the 1920s his grave was moved to Flesquieres Hill British Cemetery. The wooden cross that marked his last resting place was to be replaced with a Portland stone headstone and his father had some choice as to what information it would include. Officially his details as an ordinary soldier would have been engraved on the stone, which would have exposed the circumstances of his death. Normally there was little negotiation about the design of a stone as the whole point of the cemeteries was to create 'uniformity in death'. Perhaps because of his father's social standing as a Justice of the Peace, and maybe even because Ernest Hopcraft senior approached the Commission and explained the situation, a unique headstone was created for Ernest. It bears the badge of the 20th London Regiment, a rampart horse, and a Christian cross, along with his full name. But there is no rank and no number. At the base is an inscription which reads,

BA Jesus College Cambridge
Served as
Second Lieutenant
13th Middlesex Regiment

A casual glance on visiting the grave would certainly give the impression that Ernest Hopcraft served as an officer, and died as one, as it did to the author of this volume more than twenty years ago before the strange story of a man who went from officer to private was uncovered.

Researching Ernest Hopcraft

Officers' service records from the Great War were not stored with those of ordinary soldiers, so did not suffer the level of damage that these records did in 1940. While some were lost in later bombing, a very high percentage of officers' records survive. The file for Ernest Hopcraft was among those that did survive. None of these officers' papers have been digitised so it means a visit to TNA to see them. Regular Army and wartime-commissioned officers are found in class WO339 and Territorial officers in WO374. The Territorials are in surname order so an officer is easy to find, but WO339 is in War Office file number order. To find an officer, particularly with a common name, it is necessary to consult the name index in WO338, which is in surname order. This then gives the so-called 'Long Number' which is used to access the correct file. The WO338 index is available on microfilm at TNA, and can be downloaded for free from their Documents Online website.

Having found an officer's record what does it tell us about his service? Ernest's file was not untypical as it indicated on the front cover that at several points it had been weeded. The weeding of files was commonplace in the 1930s and often later prior to transfer into the public domain. Papers considered sensitive were often removed, or documents relating to medical treatment destroyed. The exact reasoning behind this is not clear but it does mean that almost all records are only a shadow of what they once were in terms of content. In many cases the papers in an officer's file relate to his pay and subsequent discharge, and final rank, and it can take some work and deciphering to get enough details out of the documents to help construct an outline of service. This was certainly true in the case of Ernest Hopcraft as his file was largely concerned with his subsequent dismissal rather than his actual service. One document normally always found in the file is the paper a prospective officer had to fill in giving his personal details of name, father, nationality, schooling and when and where he was born, plus the name of someone who could give him a reference. These details were used to assess that he was a British subject and therefore entitled to a commission, and to look at his educational background and references to check he was the sort of 'gentleman' suitable to become an officer. Sometimes the file contains correspondence from the officer himself, and thankfully this was the case with Ernest's record and the letter he wrote to the War Office demanding that it look again at his dismissal contained more detail on his war service than any other surviving paperwork.

His period overseas as an officer with the Middlesex Regiment and as a town major was traced using the battalion War Diary in WO95 at TNA. Some town major diaries also survive, but none for the area where he was. At one time court martial papers would have existed for his Field General Court Martial in France but they were all destroyed, possibly as late as the 1980s or 1990s, well before the explosion of interest in family history. Somewhat frustratingly it means that the exact circumstances and details of precisely what he was accused of can only be ascertained by a handful of statements in some of the documents in his service file, and this will be true of any man court-martialled in the Great War.

When Ernest Hopcraft re-enlisted as a private soldier a new record would have been started. It is quite possible he never declared his previous service as an officer, which is why no papers relating to this later period are included with it. Unfortunately, no record for him survives, and it seems likely it was lost in the Second World War. His later time overseas was therefore reconstructed from the Medal Rolls in WO329, which for the London Regiment show dates of overseas service; this confirmed that he had served both in Palestine and France in 1917–18. The 2/20th Londons'

War Diary described its movements, and the battalion was one of many that published its own private history after the war, which has now been reprinted. This was a detailed account, and gave a great insight into the circumstances of his death.

As the son of a man with money, his father was not alone in trying to memorialise him after the war, and knowing his educational background a search for Rolls of Honour for his school and university not only provided extra details, but more importantly a photograph of him. There is no central collection of these Rolls of Honour, but the Society of Genealogists Library has a good collection, as does the Imperial War Museum. If the school, college or university still exists it is always worth contacting it as it will not only have a copy of the roll, but often additional information as well.

Notes

1. Letter from Ernest Hopcraft dated March 1917 in his officer's service file TNA WO339/3775. Crown Copyright.
2. Ibid.
3. W.L. Osborn, *The History of the Seventh (Service) Battalion The Royal Sussex Regiment 1914–1919* (Times Publishing Company, 1934), p. 75.
4. A.B. Scott, *The History of the 12th (Eastern) Division in the Great War 1914–1918* (Nisbet & Co., 1923), p. 60.
5. Osborn, *The History of the Seventh (Service) Battalion*, p. 105.
6. In a letter contained in his officer's service file TNA WO339/3775.
7. Charge sheet in his officer's service file TNA WO339/3775.
8. In a letter contained his officer's service file TNA WO339/3775.
9. Ibid.
10. Ibid.
11. W.R. Elliot, *The Second Twentieth being the History of the 2/20th London Regiment* (Gale and Polden, 1920), pp. 244–5.
12. The existence of the memorial was found using the Imperial War Museum's National Inventory of War Memorials.

Chapter Eleven

BRITAIN'S BLACK PILOT –
William Robinson Clarke, Royal Flying Corps

The story of black soldiers in the British Army during the Great War is arguably one of the more neglected sides of the conflict. The concept of a large black community in Britain is often seen as a recent phenomenon, with the huge influx of people from the Caribbean in the years after the Second World War. But Edwardian Britain had a sizeable black community even then, with an estimated 20,000 black men of military age living or being resident in England by the end of the war.[1] In addition men from what were then the Colonies, the countries of the British Empire, were also resident and working in Britain; again these economic migrants are not as recent as is often believed. When war broke out in August 1914, patriotism was not just confined to the white population of Britain and the Empire. Thousands of young black men were equally keen to do their bit and enlisted to serve King and Country. Evidence shows that in Britain a large number of black men enlisted, although many had problems as the *Manual of Military Law* classed black men, or 'men of colour', as 'alien', and as such the numbers of them joining could be restricted, or the wording of the *Manual* used as a colour bar, which many found it to be. Ratu Lala Sukuna, a Fijian medical student in London, seeing his fellow interns step forward to join the Royal Army Medical Corps, attempted to do likewise but was rudely rejected. In disgust he went to France and joined the French Foreign Legion. It was not just recruiting sergeants who barred them. At the official level, Gilbert Grindle, Principal Clerk at the Colonial Office, wrote: 'I hear privately that

Robbie Clarke in Jamaica, 1914.

some recruiting officers will pass coloureds. Others, however, will not and we must discourage coloured volunteers.'[2]

The reasons behind this refusal were many and varied, and often reflected common perceptions of black people at that time. Popular culture, while it praised the warlike qualities of the many races that made up the Indian army, saw black Afro-Caribbeans as 'lazy' and a footnote in one Colonial Office paper spoke of them sleeping in hammocks all day, drinking rum. The problem of whether to accept black recruits continued throughout the war, and as late as 1917 one newspaper asked 'should our dusky warriors play a bigger part in smashing the huns?' and stated: 'we are told that the way to win the war is to turn loose millions of black men, [but] . . . it is dangerous to teach the black . . . when we have expended money and time upon the making of an army that army would be very likely to turn upon its creators'.[3] Despite these feelings many thousands of black men from Afro-Caribbean backgrounds either joined the British Army, or enlisted in the British West Indies Regiment, and they served with distinction often gaining honours and awards and battlefield promotions.

One young West Indian who joined the British Army during the Great War was William Robinson Clarke. 'Robbie' to his friends and family, he was born in Jamaica in 1895. He grew up on the south coast of the island, and although little is known about his early life, his trade in the years before the war was as a chauffeur. It was unusual enough at this time to find a man who could drive, let alone a black man, and it is possible he worked as a driver for a member of the white community in Jamaica, given they were the main owners of wheeled vehicles at that time. Whether he developed an interest in flying at this time is not known, but there was a growing interest in aviation in the West Indies in the years before the war. The first aircraft flew over the island on 21 December 1911 when an American aviator, Jesse Seligman, took to the air on a hot and windy day, watched by a crowd of more than a thousand spectators. His flight took the aircraft to more than 200ft, and he landed on a race course intact and undamaged, ready to make several more flights before he departed to follow the Panama Canal. Many thousands more came to see this and his subsequent flights; perhaps Robbie was among them?

How Robbie got to England after the outbreak of war is not known. Passage by ship was not cheap, but being a chauffeur he possibly had a little more money than the average man of his age in Jamaica. The British West Indies Regiment was forming at this time; a regiment specially raised in 1914 to allow patriotic Caribbeans to join the war effort. Indeed, one battalion began recruiting not far from his family home at Arnold Street in Kingstown. For whatever reason, Robbie never joined the British West Indies Regiment; whether he saw his skills with motor vehicles, and likely too, their mechanics, as wasted in an infantry regiment or that at this stage he was already thinking about flying, he left Jamaica and made his way to England. Here, on 26 July 1915 he joined the Royal Flying Corps for the duration of the war. He stated that his age was 19 years and 295 days, his trade was chauffeur and that he was 5ft 8½in tall. The reality of the Royal Flying Corps in 1915 was that very few men actually flew, and of those that did, most of them were officers. To keep aircraft serviceable and in the air, a huge number of ground crew were required. It was this role that Robbie went into during his first year or so as an air mechanic. His knowledge of driving and motor mechanics was almost certainly put to good use, and it is likely this is what made him an attractive recruit in the first place and possibly why they ignored the fact that he was black.

After several months' service at home he was posted to France on 18 October 1915. His service records indicate he was serving at the Royal Flying Corps Base Depot or Headquarters, and was not posted to a specific squadron at this time. This would suggest that he was probably working as a driver, possibly on the vehicles that used to go out and retrieve crashed aircraft, or as a driver for the officers of the Depot. It was a relatively uneventful time, and possibly a monotonous one. However, it did give him direct contact with flying, and one can imagine him asking questions, looking at the mechanics of the engines and equipment on the aircraft, and wishing he was able to go up in one himself. Indeed, he may well have done that. Henry Allingham, the last Great War veteran of the Royal Air Force, recalled many times that as a simple air mechanic, just like Robbie at that time, he had been given the chance to fly with a sympathetic officer. Whatever the reason, in late 1916 he made a decision to try and follow his dream of flying and put in an application for flying training. At this point in the conflict attitudes in the Royal Flying Corps were beginning to change. Flying had been the preserve largely of officers, and therefore men from a specific class background. Not only wasn't Robbie from this class he was a man of colour, which makes his acceptance onto a course for aviation instruction in December 1916 even more remarkable. He was sent to England for this training, being posted to a Training Squadron. Here he was taught the rudimentary elements of flying, not an easy task in the days before aircraft simulators. Training could be as deadly as flying in combat, and a considerable number of trainee pilots were killed or injured on their first training flight. Robbie clearly did well as a pilot as he was promoted to the rank of sergeant at the end of his training, and by May 1917 he was now ready to be posted to an active squadron in France.

On 29 May 1917 Robbie returned to France and joined 4th Squadron Royal Flying Corps at their airfield in Belgium. It was located close to the small village of Abeele, just inside the Belgian border and only a few miles from the town of Poperinghe, the major British base area on this sector of the Western Front. Beyond Poperinghe was the front line around Ypres, where the British had been fighting since October 1914. At this time the Battle of Messines was only a few days away. Tunnellers had been preparing a series of huge mines, charges of explosive, to be placed at key points along the German front line and be blown simultaneously, knocking

Now a Sergeant Pilot, Robbie Clarke just before he went to France to join 4th Squadron in 1917.

out key targets, neutralising the defences and allowing the infantry to move forward and take the Messines Ridge, which had been in German hands for three years, allowing them to dominate the battlefield south of Ypres. Royal Flying Corps squadrons had been playing a vital role in the preparations for this battle, by observing for the artillery, which would support the infantry advance with its guns, and also taking huge numbers of aerial photographs to show the state of the German trenches.

When Robbie joined them, the squadron was equipped with RE-8 aircraft. The Reconnaissance Experimental 8 was the most widely used two-seater bi-plane on the Western Front during the Great War. As its name implies, it was initially designed for aerial reconnaissance work, and it was

*Robbie Clarke in full
flying gear, pictured
with his RE8, 1917.*

used in this role when it was introduced in the autumn of 1916. But the changing use of aircraft also saw it employed as a light bomber. Being able to fly to a ceiling of 13,500ft, it was equipped with two forward-firing Vickers machine guns, and a Lewis gun on a mount in the observer's position behind the pilot. This meant it could fire on aircraft approaching it from the rear or from a flank. In the bomber role it could carry up to 260lb of bombs, which were realised by cable from under the aircraft. Robbie took to the air in one, along with his observer, in the days leading up to and during the Battle of Messines. It was only a short run from Abeele to the Messines Ridge, and although records of 4th Squadron for this period are scant, they appear to have been mainly operating in the photo-reconnaissance role. That did not mean it was not a dangerous job, as he later recalled: 'A very uncommon, though not unknown, thing happened just previously. One of our shells passed right between our planes. Both observer and myself heard it touch one of the wires. Thank goodness it did not touch the engine.'[4]

As June moved towards July, and the successful Battle of Messines at an end with the ridge now in British hands, the squadron was as busy as ever carrying out photographic missions over the battlefield south of Ypres. It was during one such mission that Robbie engaged an enemy aircraft: 'we did get one in the first scrap, which took place a couple of days before; as we saw him go down as though he was hit'.[5] A few days later he was up in the sky above the Ypres battlefield again when his luck ran out:

I had a bit of an accident day before yesterday, but will soon be alright again: so do not worry. I was doing some photographs a few miles the other side when about five Hun scouts came down upon me, and before I could get away, I got a bullet through the spine. I managed to pilot the machine nearly back to the aerodrome, but had to put her down as I was too weak to fly any more, and she was damaged in the landing as it was on bad ground. My observer escaped without any injury. I am writing this in hospital in France, but expect to escape to Blighty in a few days. Don't suppose I will do any more flying for some time.[6]

He wrote to his mother again on 7 August:

I suppose you are somewhat anxious to know how I am faring. Well, I am very much alive and kicking, though it was a near thing, and on the safe side now I am down at the base since last Saturday and in the American Hospital. They are ever so nice and look after me well,

An aerial photograph of the battlefield over Hollebeke in mid-1917 at the time Robbie Clarke was flying there.

though there are so many patients they can't spend much time on anyone in particular. I was X-Rayed yesterday morning. I do not think I will have to undergo an operation now. I feel much improved since yesterday, though very sore. The bullet passed through my spine and came out under the arm. There are also several other peculiar wounds which I cannot account for on my back, and a slight one between the eye-brows and one on my chin.[7]

The other wounds were likely to be from pieces of the aircraft fragmenting after being hit by the burst of machine-gun fire that wounded Robbie. Sections of wood and metal were likely to be flying around in every direction if the burst hit home on the aircraft, as his account suggests, and he was lucky not to have been killed. Back in England, he wrote again, this time giving a further description of what had happened.

Things were very hot when I was in France. Oh! The suffering the fellows have to bear. It is indescribable. I got my 'packet' over the

Ypres front about five miles on the German side. I was photographing, and after taking the photos, was looking out for a nice place to give Fritz a couple of pills (bombs). We were so taken up looking for a good target, that we forgot to look out for enemy scouts. The first thing I knew was hearing the rat-a-tat-tat of his machine guns, and glancing back, saw about five of them diving for me, and I could not get away in time. I was hit almost at the start of the scrap. The machine was riddled. When I was hit I was about 5,000 feet up ... I am once again in Blighty. I am getting on splendidly, felt almost fit today and am well looked after. Everything points to an early discharge from hospital.[8]

His service record shows that after he crashed he was taken back to Abeele, and from here evacuated by Ambulance Train to a General Hospital in Camiers. Close to Abeele was a large Casualty Clearing Station at a site called Remi Sidings. It is likely he was stabilised here before being put on an Ambulance Train in the sidings. He remained at Camiers for more than ten days and was then taken back to England, as he mentioned in the letter to his mother, where he was treated in hospital at Lichfield in Staffordshire. Despite playing down the nature of the wounds to his mother, he remained here until November 1917 when he was discharged and sent to a Reserve Depot of the Royal Flying Corps. Posted to light duties here, he remained at the Depot until the creation of the Royal Air Force on 1 April 1918, on which date his rank now became sergeant mechanic. Likely fed up with life at the Depot, he put in for a transfer to an active squadron but he had now been medically downgraded due to his wounds. He was posted out to the newly forming 254th Squadron Royal Air Force. This unit, based at Prawle Point in south Devon, flew DH9 bomber aircraft. These two-seater aircraft could fly to 15,000ft and the examples used by the squadron had been equipped to drop bombs suitable for knocking out submarines, as from the base in Devon they operated a coastal reconnaissance station and flew anti-submarine missions in the English Channel and along the Cornish coast.

For Robbie it was a frustrating time as he was now working as a mechanic, fixing the aircraft rather than flying them. The war ended in November 1918, and operational duties for the squadron were downgraded, so it was ironic that in January 1919 Robbie was reclassified as a sergeant pilot again. It is unlikely he flew again, however, as 254th Squadron was disbanded shortly afterwards, and Robbie found himself posted to a Repatriation Camp at Blandford in Dorset. Men like him from the Colonies who had served for Britain and survived were now in the hands of the government, who deliberated over whether they would pay for the passage of these men back to the countries they had come from. Robbie wanted to go home to his mother in Kingstown, but did not have the money to do so. A note on his service papers states that he received some good news; not only would his passage home be paid, but the original cost of coming to England would also be refunded. As with all things there would be a catch – a long wait. He remained at Blandford until August 1919 when he was given a rail warrant and sent up to Liverpool, where he boarded a ship bound for Jamaica. He was officially discharged on 24 August 1919, due to wounds and injuries acquired on active service. He was given a £60 gratuity, rather than a regular pension, which was a substantial sum in 1919, and awarded a Silver War Badge along with his three campaign medals for service on the Western Front.

Little is known of Robbie's post-war career, although he did live to into his eighties.[9] He does not appear to have ever flown again, as there was no airline and no localised air force for him to join. It is possible the injuries he suffered at Ypres precluded such a thing anyway. A generation later, thousands of Afro-Caribbeans served in the Royal Air Force during the Second World War; as pilots, air crew of Bomber Command and ground crew. But in the Great War only a handful of black men flew over the battlefields. The black American pilot Eugene Ballard is well known, and often described as the 'only black pilot of WW1'. But this was far from the truth. A handful of black pilots existed in the French air force, men from some of France's many African colonies. In the Royal Flying Corps and Royal Air Force at least two Indian-born pilots are known to have flown, but William Robinson Clarke was the only black Afro-Caribbean to have served as a pilot for Britain in the Great War. His brief career above the shell-smashed battlefields of Ypres established this young Jamaican as one of the great black aviation pioneers of the twentieth century. Ironically, close to his home in Jamaica is the country's National Heroes Park, a huge garden full of memorials to the nation's most noted sons and those who fell in two world wars. That Robbie's name should be added to this park is long overdue.

Researching William Robinson Clarke

Until the formation of the Royal Air Force in April 1918, the Royal Flying Corps was part of the British Army. For research purposes this means that the records of men who were in the RFC and/or the RAF are usually split between the Army and the Air Force. Men who served with the RFC in 1914

The veteran: home after his wound, Robbie Clarke is now wearing the ribbon of the 1914/15 Star.

and 1915 are found in the Medal Index Cards, available from TNA and online at Ancestry. Usually only details of the award of the 1914 ('Mons') Star or 1914/15 Star are recorded because these were medals issued for service with a unit then part of the Army. The other campaign medals were issued by the Air Ministry in the 1920s, and they are not noted. No RAF Medal Rolls exist for the Great War, but details of awards are noted in other documents.

The service records for men who served in either the RFC or RAF are in class AIR79 at TNA. These records are arranged by the service number of the airman concerned. This service number can be found on the Medal Index Cards if he served in the RFC in 1914/15 or on the medals themselves if they survive in the family. Otherwise, there is an alphabetical index in AIR78 where a man can be found quickly, providing his number so the record can be traced. These service records were not damaged in the Second World War and survive complete. They provide the basic information on the man himself and then details of the squadrons and units he was posted to. Dates of overseas service are shown, and as in the case of Robbie Clarke, if a man was wounded details are shown along with the medical units he was admitted to. Medals are confirmed in one section of the record, and information on discharge.

For men who flew as pilots, like Robbie Clarke, they had to have a licence issued by the Royal Aeronautical Club. These records state when the licence was issued and to whom, and include a photograph of the person concerned. A few brief details on the man are listed, along with date and place of birth, as well as profession. Ancestry digitised these and they are now available online via a simple name search.

The records of squadrons that flew in the war are in class AIR1 at TNA. Robbie Clarke's 4th Squadron lost all their records in France, and unfortunately the details of their day-to-day activities have not survived. Sometimes this can be supplemented with a published or privately published Squadron History; the Royal Air Force Museum at Hendon are worth contacting for details of these. When an aircraft engaged another in combat in the skies above the front, a form called 'Combats In The Air' had to be completed; these also survive in AIR1 but sadly are far from complete as an aviation collector stole thousands of them in the 1990s and many were never recovered.

Notes

1. D. Killingray, 'All The King's Men? Blacks in the British Army in the First World War', in I. Pegg and L. Rainer (eds), *Under The Imperial Carpet* (Rabbit Press, 1986).
2. TNA CO318/333/50043. Crown Copyright.
3. The *People*, 14 January 1917, p. 3.
4. The *Gleaner*, 9 September 1917.
5. Ibid.
6. Ibid.
7. Ibid.
8. Ibid.
9. Information on the *Gleaner* website at: www.jamaica-gleaner.com; accessed 1 March 2010.

Chapter Twelve

A POET AT WAR

Ivor Gurney, 2/5th Gloucestershire Regiment

The poetry of the Great War has in many respects become one of the strongest voices of that period. Poets such as Wilfred Owen and Edward Thomas, both of whom died in the war, and Siegfried Sassoon, who survived, are seen as key witnesses into the horror and perceived futility of the conflict. While no one would deny the horror that was the Great War, many modern historians have been critical of some of these voices because the majority of the war poets were wealthy, from specific class backgrounds and served in the trenches as officers. Such historians argue that because of this they are hardly representative of the majority of men who fought in the war. One man recognised as one of the war poets but who came from a very different background to Owen, Sassoon and Thomas was Ivor Gurney; he served in the ranks, was wounded twice but survived the war.

Ivor Bertie Gurney was born at 3 Queen Street, Gloucester, in August 1890. His father David was a tailor who had married Florence, and together they had four children of which Ivor was the second; he had an elder sister, and a younger brother and sister. Queen Street, demolished before the Second World War, was a small terraced house typical of the cramped Victorian buildings in the area. David Gurney had his own shop, in which his wife assisted him, and while they were far from being a wealthy family, they were not destitute either and were typical of many Victorian families with middle-class aspirations. Indeed, they later moved to a more respectable part of Gloucester with a house that doubled as the family shop.

Religion was very much part of the Gurney household, and they all worshipped at the local All Saints' Church. Here Ivor Gurney first came into serious contact with music, which would feature strongly throughout the rest of his life as he became a choir boy at the church. His great ability to sing won him a place in the Gloucester Cathedral choir from 1900 to 1906, where he became a pupil at the King's School. Passionate about music, he began composing at the age of 14 and in 1911 won a scholarship to the Royal College of Music, where he studied under the same tutor who taught Ralph Vaughan Williams among others.

Ivor Gurney, 1915. (Ivor Gurney Estate)

The Great War interrupted his studies, although he appears to have been on a walking holiday in rural Gloucestershire in the summer of 1914, a place and a landscape he was increasingly recognising as both his spiritual home and inspiration for his work as a composer and poet. Gurney had been wearing glasses for some years, and it appears that when he tried to enlist in 1914 he was turned down because of poor eyesight. By February 1915 the number of volunteers was beginning to dry up, and medical examiners were not as fussy as when the first appeal for men had gone out in 1914. Ivor Gurney tried again and on 9 February 1915 joined the 5th Battalion Gloucestershire Regiment as a Territorial soldier. This was the local unit, which had expanded to three battalions with one about to depart for France, a second – known as 2/5th Battalion – which Ivor was posted to and a third one to act as a reserve for the other two.

The 2/5th had been formed in September 1914 and Ivor joined it at the point it was moving from Gloucester for further training in Northampton. 'Northampton gave the men their first experience of being billeted in a strange Borough: it also afforded the Battalion its first lessons in training as a part of a large unit.'[1] Training was fairly rudimentary at this stage and largely consisted of physical drill, route marches and bayonet and rifle practice. Due to the huge influx of volunteers in 1914 and 1915 the War Office could not equip the Army with the up-to-date 1908 Pattern webbing equipment that soldiers used to carry their rifle ammunition and personal gear. They therefore introduced an emergency set of equipment known as the 1914 Pattern leather equipment. A leather belt with a snake buckle, leather cross straps and box ammunition pouches, it supported the carrying of bayonet, entrenching tool, water bottle, a haversack and under certain circumstances a large pack as well. Rushed into production, it was not as comfortable as webbing, especially on long marches. But sets of it were issued in their thousands and Ivor's battalion was equipped with it at this stage. He found the training tough, but later wrote: 'here I am, a soldier of the King, and the best thing for me – at present. I feel that nowhere could I be happier than where I am . . . so the experiment may be called a success. What the future holds has to be kept out of sight.'[2]

The remainder of 1915 was spent in Essex, working on the trenches that formed the outer defences of London. At this stage in the war the fear of invasion was still a reality, or at least a perceived reality, especially following the naval bombardment of Scarborough in 1914 and the increasing use of Zeppelins. While the War Office never saw invasion as a serious proposition, given the Royal Navy's command of the sea, it felt the preparation of such defences worthwhile and it gave home-service troops like Ivor Gurney and the 2/5th Battalion something to work on. Proper training then followed on Salisbury Plain, and by this stage the battalion was part of the 61st (South Midland) Division. A Territorial formation, its

Men of the 2/5th Gloucestershire Regiment in training, 1916.

three Brigades were made up of troops from not just the Gloucestershire Regiment, but units recruited in Berkshire and Oxfordshire, and also the Royal Warwickshires and Worcestershire Regiment. On Salisbury Plain they trained as a division for the first time, and Ivor and his comrades gradually came into more and more contact with the other units and the men in them.

As 1915 moved into 1916 it seemed that the 2/5th and the entire Division might be destined for home service for the remainder of the war. But events on the Western Front, and at Gallipoli and in Salonika in 1915 had stretched the resources of the War Office and more and more units were required for the front. The spring of 1916 saw numerous formations carrying out reserve duties or home service dispatched for France, and on 24 May 1916 Ivor Gurney and the men of his battalion left for Southampton to join those who had already gone.

> A bugle sound the 'fall in'. Men and officers came tumbling out of huts on to the parade ground, laden with the accoutrements of war. The anticipation of a change and the feeling of a new importance made them unconscious of their resemblance to well-stocked Christmas trees. Ranks were dressed, rolls were checked and then the troops stood easy waiting for the moment of departure. The routine remark 'all present and correct, sir' broke the spell. Many a time before the same words had been uttered, but now they seemed to bear a new significance. Who, it was wondered, would be present when the roll was called on some not far distant date? What names would fall on ears so deaf that not even the sternest command would rouse them to respond?[3]

Arriving at Le Havre, the battalion immediately went into a rest camp and from there proceeded to the front by train. A long march from the railhead brought the battalion to a shattered village close to the trenches, and along with it the realisation that they were now at war. One officer of the battalion recalled the following sentiment at this time: 'Whatever may be said about the futility of war, it reawakened human sympathies that had become numbed through disuse; it brought romance into a complacent age; it fused the masses into a common purpose; through it youth was justified and by it older men were rejuvenated. To have taken part in the war is indeed to have thought great thoughts and to have lived till we proved them true.'[4]

By this stage of the conflict Ivor Gurney was serving in the battalion signal section. There was no Corps of Royal Signals in the Great War. Signalling was split between infantry signallers like Ivor at battalion level,

Gurney, now a signaller, photographed with his company just prior to going to France. (Ivor Gurney Estate)

and the Royal Engineers who operated at Divisional level and above. His signal section were responsible for ensuring that communications between all the command dugouts in the battalion's sector were kept open, and establishing signal relay posts where they could signal back to the Royal Engineers or other units if required. In the trenches the most common form of communication was telephones connected on fixed cables, normally pinned to the sides of the trench. These required constant maintenance as even a tiny shell fragment could break them. If the telephone system broke down, which could often happen, Ivor and his comrades would be required to signal using electric Lucas signalling lamps, heliographs or even flags. All this sort of work put signallers at great risk and in major battles their life expectancy was short. Thankfully, the sector they were moving into, close to the village of Laventie, was part of the so-called 'quiet' area of the battlefield, where no major operations were taking place and where battalions fresh from England could acclimatise to the conditions of the trenches. The battalion history describes the first journey into the labyrinth:

> After meeting guides from the London Welsh . . . the troops moved up to the trenches. That night is one of vivid memories – the curious names of the lanes, Eton Road, Cheltenham Road, Rugby Road – then the main road running from Estaires to La Bassée – then Rouge Croix

with its red Crucifix and the sentry standing at the cross-roads, then, after a long wait the splitting up into small parties and proceeding at intervals along a duckboarded trench – the Verey lights in the near distance, the tat-tat of machine-guns and the occasional whistle of a stray bullet and the instinct to duck. The village of Neuve-Chapelle lay on the right. A further twenty minutes and Sign Post Lane was reached and then the front line breastworks. The night was very dark and the Verey lights from both sides lit up everything at intervals in a ghostly sort of way; there was, too, an uncanny stillness in the air, broken occasionally by some spasmodic firing. It was difficult to imagine that this place had any connection with a world war – it seemed so quiet.[5]

Neuve-Chapelle had been the site of heavy fighting in 1915, but since that time the front had been as quiet as described in this account, save the activity of tunnellers from both sides working beneath the battlefield. The front of the 2/5th Battalion was indeed littered with mine craters, but Ivor Gurney's duties as a signaller meant that he did not need to be in the front line all the time. Generally, in a well-constructed trench system like this, on a static front, the infrastructure of the battlefield was well laid out. As signallers carried a lot of equipment they needed a place to keep their stores, cable and tools. Usually they would be allocated a dugout or shelter somewhere close to the second-line trenches, so they could be on hand to react immediately to breakages. Somewhere in the second or third line, possibly in a smashed farm building, there would also be their signal relay station which was rear facing – facing towards positions behind the lines – so that they could signal to another battalion relay post further back or even the Divisional Signal Company. The work of the signallers was ably described in the 2/5th Battalion's history:

The scene . . . is Headquarters Signal Office . . . The operator receives a report from A Company, who are holding the front line, of heavy enemy shelling; he communicates the message to the Commanding Officer who asks to be put through to the company; the operator plugs in, but gets no reply. The line has been broken. A Corporal and a linesman prepare to go along to A Company's line; they dash up the steps of the dugout and dive into the trench to wallow knee deep in slush. After plunging along for fifty yards, the linesman taps in and calling Battalion is answered immediately; the break is further afield – they must go on. Presently the line disappears over the top and they

Laventue church, visited by Ivor Gurney in 1916.

follow out into the open ground where their only shelter from
continuous gun fire is water-logged shell holes. They scramble on,
holding the telephone line for guidance until ahead of them they can
dimly see the white outline of [a] trench. There is the screaming

sound of a shell and they drop into the nearest shell hole just as, with a blinding flash, the earth ten yards ahead is churned up; they rush into the trench, tap in again and again are answered by Battalion, but still there is no reply from A Company. On they must go again, out into the open . . . evidently this is where the line is broken. Ultimately after much stumbling, searching and a few comments on shells and Germans in general, one broken end is found and then the other, some forty or fifty yards away. The two men now crouch in a pot hole and join the ends; a phone, which the linesman always carries with him, is connected and at last A Company is spoken to. It looks as though their task is now done, but alas! It is now found that no reply is forthcoming from Battalion – another breakage – two more loose ends to be found and repaired – more comments on shells and Germans.[6]

Between tours in the trenches carrying out work like this and periods of rest at small villages close to the front, Ivor Gurney had a gradual introduction to the war. The only major episode during Gurney's time here was the attack on Fromelles on 19 July 1916. The 61st Division attacked alongside the 5th Australian Division, and two days' fighting cost them nearly 8,000 combined casualties. The 2/5th Gloucesters were not directly involved, but were in reserve and watched the tragedy unfold. More than ninety years later the remains of hundreds of those who died in this battle have been found by archaeologists and will be buried in the first new Great War cemetery to be constructed since the 1930s.

His work as a signaller, while dangerous, meant that there were also long periods of no activity which gave him time to sit and contemplate, and to work on poems and music. He made good use of this time, and periods out of the line, and work began on a collection of poems that would result in his first published volume of war poetry entitled *Severn & Somme*. This volume, later published in 1917, drew on his work as a signaller and in one poem, 'The Signaller's Vision', he recalls:

> One rainy winter dusk,
> Mending a parted cable,
> Sudden I saw so clear
> Home and the tea table.[7]

The title of the volume with its reference to the Somme reflects the movement of his battalion from the Laventie–Fromelles front down to the Somme at the end of the battle. By this stage major attacks were still going

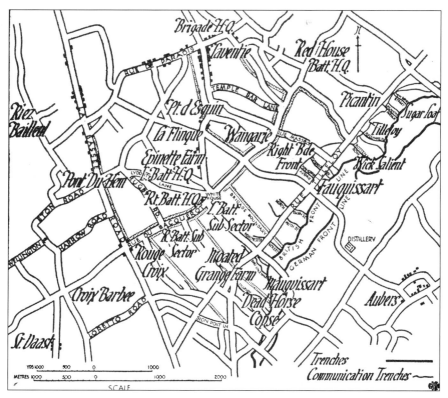

Map of the battlefield occupied by the 2/5th Glosters in 1916.

on, but Gurney's battalion would not participate in them. Instead, they found themselves thrown into the attritional nature of the battle, holding ground north of the village of Courcelette around Regina Trench. The October rains on the Somme, combined with the terrific shelling, had turned the battlefield into a quagmire and made the job of signallers like Ivor all the more difficult, and daily existence in the front line far from pleasant. The battalion history later recalled: 'here were primitive conditions – men clinging to shell holes, mud deep enough to completely submerge a gun team and limber, masses of unburied dead strewn over the battlefields; no sign of organised trenches, but merely shell holes joined up to one another – and . . . no landmarks anywhere. The whole scene was one bleak wilderness of death.'[8]

Ivor used poetry to forget what he saw before him on a daily basis and later wrote in 'Trees':

The dead land oppressed me;
I turned my thoughts away,
And went where hill and meadow
Are shadowless and gay.[9]

He was hardly alone as a soldier in a strange country, smashed to bits by the hand of war, to turn to thoughts of home, fields and woods he once knew. Where Gurney was different was that he expressed it in verse, and one can almost sense the terror in many of his words at times.

Following the extremely cold winter of 1916/17 the German army planned to withdraw from the Somme front, and this was put into effect in March 1917 during the so-called Withdrawal to the Hindenburg Line. This latter named system of defences had been constructed by the Germans during that winter so they had a new and what they hoped was an impregnable line to pull back to. The 2/5th found itself on the move and engaging in a very different type of warfare – open movement. The mire of Courcelette and Regina Trench was left behind, and instead were the open fields along the Amiens–St Quentin road in the area where the Somme met the Aisne. In the sector allocated to the 2/5th Glosters the Germans were putting up a defence around the village of Bihecourt. The battalion attacked them on 2 April 1917 and the village was taken. The battalion dug in at an orchard on the far side, and on 7 April B and C Companies pushed forward from the orchard towards the German trenches' site close to the village of Fayet on the high ground beyond. According to his service record, Ivor Gurney was wounded here on 7 April, with a Gun Shot Wound to the right arm. It is likely this was from wild rifle or machine-gun fire as he advanced with his signalling equipment, accompanying the attacking infantry companies, over the open ground towards the village; ground that is just as open and coverless ninety years later. While any wound is serious, Ivor's took him as far as the Base Hopsital at Rouen. It wasn't a 'Blighty One' – a wound serious enough to get a soldier back home to England. And unbeknown to him, fellow war poet Wilfred Owen was only a few fields away at Savy with the 2nd Manchesters at exactly the same time.

Upon recovery he was posted to an Infantry Base Depot in Rouen and by late May was back with his battalion, now in the Arras area. The many biographies of Gurney state that at this point he left the 2/5th Battalion Gloucestershire Regiment and transferred to the 184th Company Machine Gun Corps. The Machine Gun Corps was a specialist unit of the British Army formed in October 1915 to utilise machine guns, which were now becoming an increasingly important weapon in trench warfare. Each

Ivor Gurney at Rouen, 1917.
(Ivor Gurney Estate)

Infantry Brigade had its own company, which took the number of that Brigade; 184th Company being part of 184th Infantry Brigade, 61st (South Midland) Division, which also included the 2/5th Glosters. His service record appears to contradict this to some extent, as it mentions no transfer to the Machine Gun Corps and nor do his medal records. If a transfer had taken place he would have been issued with a new number and reference to the transfer would have been made in these two sources. It seems more likely that given his specialist skills as a signaller, he was attached to the 184th Company to continue with those duties. Indeed, this appears to be confirmed in some of the letters he sent home. His attachment would have taken him away from the close-knit 'family' of his battalion signal section into a unit full of strangers, although his day-to-day tasks are unlikely to have been very different except that machine-gun companies generally did not stay in the front line long, and moved about more frequently minimising the chances of the gun being discovered and fired upon by the enemy.

By July 1917 he had moved with his new unit, which according to the War Diary and also Gurney's letters, seems to have been permanently attached to support the 2/5th Battalion Gloucestershire Regiment, to another new sector – Ypres. Ypres had been the centre of British operations on the Western Front since October 1914. Following the Second Battle of Ypres the Germans had captured the majority of the high ground and commanded the battlefield for the next two years until events at Messines and Passchendaele changed that. Conditions here were appalling:

> a desolate pock-marked area, ripped to pieces by gun fire almost since the commencement of the war. All drainage was destroyed and the advent of rain at once turned the whole place into one vast bog of pestilential slime and filth. It was across this plain that the advance on Passchendaele had to be made. Duckboard tracks were laid and along these the men moved in single file. To slip off these tracks, as sometimes happened at night, often meant drowning in slime; to remain on them was almost as perilous since the German guns had every track taped.[10]

The offensive began on 31 July 1917, but Gurney's unit was not involved. There was initially some success that day, but in the evening it began to rain and barely stopped for many weeks to come, increasing the problems associated with the conditions already described. And despite the success, it was not without casualties. One of those who died on 31 July was Francis Ledwidge. Ledwidge was arguably Ireland's most important twentieth-century poet; he had joined as a volunteer in 1914, served at Gallipoli and in Salonika, and had only been on the Western Front a few months. Ivor Gurney had been a great admirer of Ledwidge and wrote: 'so Ledwidge is dead . . . He was a true poet, and the story of his life is (now) a sad but romantic tale, like that of so many others, so wastefully spent. Yet the fire may not have been struck in them save for the war; anyway it was to be, and is.'[11] The news was received by Gurney when his unit was in a captured German trench at St Julien, just north-east of Ypres, and only a few miles from where Ledwidge had been killed and was buried. Gurney could not have known that, but his death must have made him reflect on his own mortality, and his chances of survival.

By September 1917 the fighting had moved beyond St Julien, the rain had barely subsided and Gurney's unit and the 2/5th Glosters had been in and out of the line, suffering casualties from the attritional nature of the battle until they had participated in an attack close to a ruined agricultural

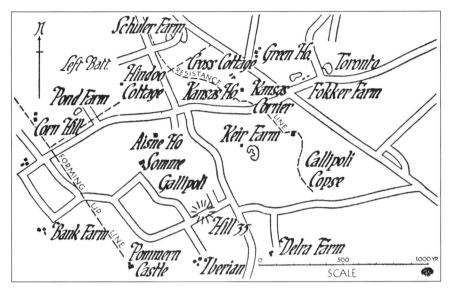

Map of the battlefield where Ivor Gurney was gassed in September 1917.

settlement called Pond Farm on British trench maps. Here on 22 August an attack had been launched and Gurney had been assisting in fatigue duties bringing up equipment and ammunition to the machine-gun positions. The Germans had retaliated with heavy shell fire, and he had been hit twice by shrapnel; on the belt and on his helmet. Neither impact had wounded him, but letters home show he was shocked by it. These sort of details were not recorded in service records, and it is only through surviving letters that we are aware of it.

The next date that features in Gurney's official papers is 10 September 1917. On this day he is recorded as having been wounded in action by a gas shell. He later wrote: 'I am out of it for a day or two, gassed in the throat 5 days ago – but not thinking to get anything out of it. How long will it last? Couldn't say, but not so long as I would wish. Being gassed (mildly) with the new gas is no worse than catarrh or a bad cold.'[12] But it was much more serious than catarrh. The gassing had taken place in a quiet period, when the 184th Company Machine Gun Corps, supporting the 2/5th Battalion Gloucestershire Regiment in the trenches, had moved up from a reserve position on the Yser Canal, north of Ypres, to prepare for an attack. They had taken over positions around an area marked as 'Somme' on the maps;

Pond Farm, or what was left of it, 1917.

Gas! A group of signallers in the midst of a gas attack, Ypres, 1917.

all the farms here had the names of battles such as Aisne, Gallipoli and Somme. The Somme position included several concrete structures, and the maps show three small farm buildings here along with the wreck of a British tank. Ahead of them was a piece of rising ground known as Hill 35, and beyond that in the far distance the ridges around the village of Passchendaele were also visible. The attack was eventually called off, and instead the men found themselves working on improving the trench system in the area; no mean feat in an area resembling a swamp where digging any sort of hole usually saw it full of water in minutes. Gurney would have found himself based in one of the ruins or the concrete bunkers, carrying out his signalling duties for the machine-gun teams supporting the infantry.

On 10 September a fresh bombardment brought gas shells among the usual high explosives. The Somme farm complex was only a mile or so from where gas had been used for the first time in April 1915. Then gas had been released from cylinders forming a gas cloud which depended on the wind to carry it. Now the weapon was more sophisticated; it could be delivered in shells and new types of gas were being developed, and increasingly more and more deadly. By this stage British soldiers like Ivor Gurney were issued with Small Box Respirators; a proper form of gas mask that fitted to the face, and through which the man breathed. A tube connected the mask to a filter, but it often took a while for replacement filters to be issued when new enemy gasses were introduced. Whether this was the case on 10 September or whether Gurney didn't get his mask on in time is impossible to say, but he was gassed far more severely than his letter implies. His wound took him back not just to a Field Ambulance and Casualty Clearing Station, but base hospital and then back to England on 23 September 1917. Gas wounds were often debilitating, affecting the soldier's throat and lungs. Some men quickly recovered and were sent back to active service, but for others it was the start of an unrecoverable decline. Gurney fell into that category, and while for official purposes he was posted to a reserve battalion of the Gloucestershire Regiment, in reality he spent the next year in a succession of hospitals. By September 1918 the Army officially medically downgraded him, and following a final medical inspection deemed that he would never be fit for service again. He was therefore discharged 'no longer fit for war service' on 4 October 1918. His war from Severn to the Somme to Passchendaele had come to an end.

For Ivor Gurney, however, while his direct involvement in the war was over, the memories of it, and its dominance of his life, was not. His health

An aerial photograph of the ground where Ivor Gurney was gassed, showing how few recognisable features were left by this stage of the battle.

was permanently affected by the gas and the memories of the war not only populated his music and poetry, they increasingly populated his state of mind, which gradually declined. By 1922 he was declared insane and spent much of the rest of his life in and out of mental asylums. The war, and the memories of it, had consumed him. Eventually he became physically as well as mentally ill, and died of tuberculosis on 26 December 1937, aged 47.

Gurney appears in no casualty list of the Great War, but he was as much as casualty of it as the men he served alongside who died on the field of battle. Perhaps he would have concluded of himself the same comments he made of Francis Ledwidge: 'Yet the fire may not have been struck in them save for the war'? And certainly his legacy and voice, a voice from the ranks of ordinary soldiers, makes him arguably one of the most important Great War poets and writers.

Researching Ivor Gurney

Researching someone who is a well-known figure might at first appear quite simple. There are numerous biographies of Ivor Gurney, and it would be easy to assume that all the information required to research his war service would be found in them. However, the majority were written before the availability of the Medal Index Cards and service records, and a quick search of them showed that when it came to the specifics of where he served and when, they were not only contradictory, but often not very sure when certain things had happened. What they did do was provide insights into the man himself and how the war affected him; something not normally found in conventional research into a Great War soldier.

Ivor Gurney's final wound in 1917, when he was gassed, effectively ended his war and led to a medical discharge from the Army before the war was over. As he later received a pension for this, his papers were found in WO364 at TNA in the so-called 'Pension Papers'. The file was not complete as some documents had no doubt been removed as irrelevant to his claim for a pension, but they provided the basic details of his enlistment, training, postings, service overseas and when he was wounded. This information contradicted much of what was contained in his biographies, and showed that he had been wounded twice; once on the Hindenburg Line and once at Ypres, when he was gassed. The service record also clearly confirmed that he had never been transferred to the Machine Gun Corps, which all his biographies state, and that he was only attached to them.

To follow his war service the battalion War Diary was of use, but of greater help was the privately published battalion history of the 2/5th Glosters. This gives a great insight into where Gurney trained, where he served in Northern France and on the Somme, and where he was wounded. The history is unusually well written and rather than just a collection of places, dates and deeds, it gives reflections on what it was like to be there and has good notes on the role of signallers, whom Gurney served with in the battalion.

Notes

1. A.F. Barnes, *The Story of the 2/5th Battalion Gloucestershire Regiment 1914–1918* (The Crypt House Press, 1930), p. 19.
2. Quoted in M. Hurd, *The Ordeal of Ivor Gurney* (Oxford University Press, 1978), p. 54.
3. Barnes, *The Story of the 2/5th Battalion Gloucestershire Regiment*, p. 32.
4. Ibid., p. 36.
5. Ibid., p. 37.
6. Ibid., pp. 56–7.
7. I. Gurney, *Severn & Somme* (Sidgwick & Jackson, 1917).
8. Barnes, *The Story of the 2/5th Battalion Gloucestershire Regiment*, p. 53.
9. Gurney, *Severn & Somme*.
10. Barnes, *The Story of the 2/5th Battalion Gloucestershire Regiment*, pp. 68–9.
11. R.K.R. Thornton, *Ivor Gurney: War Letters* (Hogarth Press, 1984), pp. 185–6.
12. Ibid., p. 199.

FURTHER READING

Bridger, Geoff, *The Great War Handbook*, Pen & Sword, 2009

Brooks, Richard, *Tracing Your Royal Marine Ancestors*, Pen & Sword, 2008

Doyle, Peter, *The British Soldier of the First World War*, Shire, 2008

——, *British Army Cap Badges of the First World War*, Shire, 2010

Duckers, Peter, *British Campaign Medals 1914–2005*, Shire, 2006

Dymond, Steve, *Researching British Military Medals*, Crowood Press, 2007

Fowler, Simon, *Tracing Your Army Ancestors*, Pen & Sword, 2006

——, *Tracing Your First World War Ancestors*, Countryside Books, 2008

Holding, Norman and Swinnerton, Iain, *Location of British Army Records: A National Directory of World War I Sources*, FFHS, 1999

——, *World War I Army Ancestry*, FFHS, 2004

Pappalardo, Bruno, *Tracing Your Naval Ancestors*, PRO Publications, 2003

Spencer, William, *First World War Army Service Records: A Guide for Family Historians*, TNA, 2008

——, *Air Force Records: A Guide for Family Historians*, TNA, 2008

INDEX